the miraculous laws of

universal

dynamics

al g. manning

THE MIRACULOUS LAWS OF

prentice-hall, inc., englewood cliffs, n.j.

UNIVERSAL

DYNAMICS

▼

FIFTH PRINTING . . . . JUNE, 1968

To Michael and Richard

—may they walk in the light, always.

How
This Book
Will Help
You

Have you ever had the gnawing inside you that causes you to say, "I'm hungry, but I don't know what I want"? Yet you know it isn't a physical hunger. Have you ever experienced that feeling of restlessness which makes you wonder what it all means, whether life is worth the effort it takes to live it? If so, you are expressing the inner needs of man—needs which lead him to seek out the hidden laws that govern *life*. It was just such a drive that led me to the years of personal research and "field testing" in business and private life, the results of which are summarized in these pages.

The energy, the force that drives life, is a totally dynamic system of laws that operate here and everywhere, now and for all time. All we need do is learn these Miraculous Laws to answer the unspoken questions within ourselves, to soothe the pains that come from "drifting" through this life, to relieve the hunger for life that plagues every man at one time or another.

Seek and Find

In this book you will learn that every material need will always be met, but you will also gain the wisdom to know that rewards cannot be measured in monetary terms alone. You will learn how to *truly* enrich your life by following laws that man is now ready to receive again—simple laws that will bring you inner peace, confidence, and power. You will ascend to a new realization that within yourself you can attain the "peace that passeth all understanding" and that you have the *power to achieve* your heart's desire.

For many long years, I delved into and sifted through the philosophies, the Mystery Schools, the great religions of the East and the West, theories of great men like Freud, Adler, Jung—and on into the night. In the pragmatism of William James there is a lesson that proved to be the key for me. It is, simply, if something works well and consistently, use it! And don't worry about why it works. This is a first step in learning and applying the Laws of Universal Dynamics—laws that can literally work miracles in your life if you let them. In this life we must be practical, and as practical people we need tools that work well. Our only concern should be to make our life-tools work better, so that our lives are fuller, richer and better in every way. This book shows you how to pick the right tools and how to use them well.

All the Time and Everywhere

An important part of this book will center on the practical. This in itself is a source of peace, a way out of the dark forest of despair. You might compare it to getting your television set properly tuned. Now you can see what's going on!

In this book you will learn how to eliminate confusion,

illusion, and delusion from your life. By the practical process of testing in the field of life, you make each theory prove itself. You test every theory in the dynamic laboratory of life, and you emerge with new knowledge, new power of understanding, and you progress upward. When you test every theory, you will find what works for you and what doesn't. If it doesn't work for you, discard it! When you thus eliminate the dross, you lay bare the few, simple, practical principles by which our tiny portion of the universe functions. By applying the simple, yet little-known, Laws of Universal Dynamics, you will be able to avoid wasting time and life, and you will immediately begin to start living practically and fruitfully. By following the program outlined in this book you will truly learn how to get the most out of your life.

This book will show you how to keep life from slipping by unused. By practicing the principles clearly spelled out for you, results are assured you, and the amazing part of it is that *you* set the goals, *you* decide what the results will be, for nothing will be beyond your reach.

This book is written by a man who has made his share of mistakes in the world, just as everyone has. In fact, since no one has yet reached the state of perfection, I may make more mistakes—you might too, so, above all things, do not get discouraged. The important thing to remember is that we must wring every ounce of livingness out of this life, and the next one too. This book will show you how.

My purpose in writing this book has been to bring you power, confidence, peace, and joy, because I *know* that you can attain these things if you only try, if you only give your attention and your "will-to-do" to the program outlined for you and to the Miraculous Laws of Universal Dynamics.

Begin now to receive your share!

Contents

5. *how to develop personal electromagnetism*   **79**

Why balanced growth is essential. How to tap your magnetic force. The secret switch. Trigger your secret switch
daily. Meet each person on his own level. Review the
steps.

6. *utilizing the magic pyramid for eternal peace of mind*   **93**

Build faith with knowledge. Learn to follow the middle
path. Gaining true growth through the pyramid of seesaws. Don't beat yourself. Let God handle the timing.

7. *learn the secret of life balance*   **105**

Know the importance of good timing. Understand the
value of discipline. Enjoy the game of life. How to control your temper. Overcoming boredom. Full life-
enjoyment.

8. *let the growth machine make you important*   **121**

How to put service to work for you. How to operate
your growth machine. How the law of attraction and
repulsion acts. Never try to steal growth. Personal
importance.

9. *how to turn every acquaintance into a true friend*   **131**

Look for growth. How to warm your acquaintanceships.
How to build an elementary friendship. How to share
infinite love. How to transfer the rapport to God. Live
outwardly.

How to
Grasp and Use
the Secret of Greatness

From Africa and Europe to the Americas, ancient man left awesome relics of a secret power. Massive works of stone still stand, structures so tremendous that today's finest construction equipment could not tackle such a task. Were the pyramids of Egypt really

chapter one

built by thousands of man-years of slave labor? Or, were they built with the aid of a mighty power held secret in the hearts of men?

Answer the question and lay it aside for now. In our final chapter we will ask it again and compare your two answers. If you assimilate the ideas presented in this work and let them become a living part of your being, you will find your second answer full of meaning and practical value. This will be the result of your own *personal experience*.

Here's Help for You, Now!

A man had just watched his life savings go down the drain in an unsuccessful business venture. He encountered these ideas and quickly understood what had caused his failure. He started again, with a determination to apply his new knowledge. Today he is worth two million dollars and well on his way to the third.

A woman had been "sentenced" to a wheel chair for the rest of her life. But something within her rebelled. She applied these principles and in six weeks was able to take her first halting steps. Now she walks straight and tall and has returned to the active, useful life she was told she had lost.

The express purpose of this book is to cause *you,* the reader, to enjoy a new *personal experience* and gain the *power* to achieve health, wealth, happiness, peace of mind, love, and anything else you may desire. Of course there is a price! It is your discovery and use of a secret.

Down through the ages, knowledge of this secret and its proper application has given men full, happy, prosperous, and meaningful lives. Men who misunderstood or misapplied it have led lives of pain, misery, and despair. All the great men of history have used it, whether consciously or unconsciously. And any great man of the future will derive his power and strength from the same source.

In the history of our country, George Washington, Abraham Lincoln, and Robert E. Lee used it properly. Benedict Arnold, John Wilkes Booth, and Aaron Burr misapplied it. We will call it the *secret of greatness*.

Let's understand from the beginning: we are not going to teach you how to get something for nothing. Our universe just doesn't work that way! By proper application of these principles you may get *rich*—you may even "get rich quick"—but you will earn it.

A great Teacher once said, "It is your Father's good pleasure to give you the Kingdom."

Is that something for nothing?

To those who answer yes: that *yes* answer is *why* you have the nothing. The trick lies in the word *Father*. Does a father give his young child something for nothing?

No! He gives to the youngster *for being his child*. And the scope of the gift is limited to the youngster's capacity to use it, rather than the parent's capacity to give. This is a deep basic principle and should be understood carefully. The Universe has an infinite capacity to give to you, but you must develop *your capacity* to receive and *use* its gifts. The Secret of Greatness will bring about this development, just as it has for the leaders of all ages.

Mining Your Treasury of Power

Over four thousand years ago, the great teachers of men used a *power* to perform wondrous works far beyond the imagination of modern man. The first part of the Secret of Greatness is:

The Power has never been lost to the world. It lies hidden deep within you!

You use part of it every second of your life. In fact, it is the very *life* within you. But unfortunately, most of us use only a tiny fraction of the power available because we just don't know any better. By learning to use more of your hidden Power you will bring a measure of improvement to all men as you begin to get the most out of life.

A boy received a fox terrier puppy for his tenth birthday. It was a lively, loving little dog, but where its right ear should have been there was only a tiny ridge of skin. They became devoted pals immediately, but the boy didn't want his dog to "look funny." Every morning before school he worked with the pup. He hugged and petted it, and talked to it like another child. "All puppies have two ears," he said. "You can grow your other one if you want to. Please do it for me."

He never missed his session, no matter what else he was going to do, and in six months that pup had two perfect ears. A little child used his hidden power with faith and determination. So can you.

How to Use the First Secret

Here is the first secret. Learn to use a little more of your Hidden Power each day as you strive to realize your heart's desires. Learn that true happiness comes only from growth, or what you might prefer to call progress. This can be purely personal, or part of group progress. But without it, there is no lasting joy.

Assume that suddenly all your fondest wishes and dreams

came true. Would you be happy? Naturally! But for how long? In a few days or weeks you would come up with a whole new set of desires and goals. The old restlessness would return and you would feel, "I'm right back where I started from."

A young man started working his way through college as a bus boy. By hard work and careful planning he was barely managing. The self-discipline was rigorous, but he kept his mind on the goal and worked happily. When he unexpectedly inherited a large sum of money, he thought his struggle was over so he "let down." As a result of not applying himself he flunked three courses. The disappointment helped bring him to the profound realization that life without challenge and struggle is death in disguise. He again accepted the challenge of his studies and eventually gained a Ph.D.

Lasting happiness comes only from the feeling of steady progress toward worthwhile goals. In all of nature you see the law of growth in action. Everything is either growing or in a state of decay. There is no standing still! And so it is with you. You must grow or be left behind by the progress of the rest of the world. This feeling of losing ground, deep in the heart of your being, is the seat of all unhappiness.

How to Start Using the Power of the Secret

How can you use the Secret of Greatness within you to bring orderly growth and its resultant happiness into your life now? The answer we seek must be practical. We want it to work *every time* we use it.

Our understanding comes from the nature and operation of the Hidden Power itself:

The Hidden Power in you is the same force that created

and sustains the universe. To use it for self-improvement you must understand its purpose and cooperate with it.

Modern science says the Power which created the universe operates through the principle of evolution. We are told that life on earth started with single cells in the sea. In time they evolved into plants, fish, amphibians, reptiles, mammals, and finally man himself. The gaps between the species are explained as mutations, or freaks, born to other species. Nature provides for progress by the Law of Natural Selection, or the survival of the fittest. The strongest and most intelligent grow greater, while the weaker perish.

In human society we often hear this voiced as the ancient complaint, "Them as has, gets!"

The Master put it, ". . . *it is given unto you to know the mysteries of the Kingdom of Heaven, but to them it is not given. For whosoever hath, to him shall be given, and he shall have more abundance: but whosoever hath not, from him shall be taken away even that he hath.*" (Matt. 13:11-12)

When Darwin published his theory of evolution, many thought it disproved Christianity. What short sightedness! We just quoted Jesus on evolution. The Master taught it naturally and fluently 2,000 years ago.

Consider this parable of Christ:

> For the Kingdom of Heaven is as a man traveling into a far country, who called his own servants, and delivered unto them his goods. And unto one he gave five talents, to another two, and to another one.
>
> Then he that had received the five talents went and traded with the same, and made five other talents. And likewise he that had received two, he also gained other two. But he that had received one went and digged in the earth, and hid his lord's money.
>
> After a long time the lord of those servants cometh,

and reckoneth with them. And so he that had received five talents came and brought other five talents. . . . His lord said unto him, well done, thou good and faithful servant: thou hast been faithful over a few things: I will make thee ruler over many things: enter thou into the joy of thy lord.

He also that had received two talents came and said, . . . behold I have gained two other talents beside them. His lord said unto him, Well done. . . .

Then he which had received the one talent came and said, Lord, I knew thee that thou art an hard man, reaping where thou hast not sown . . . and I was afraid, and went and hid thy talent in the earth: lo, there thou hast that is thine. His lord answered . . . Thou wicked and slothful servant, thou knewest that I reap where I sowed not . . . Thou oughtest therefore to have put my money to the exchangers, and then at my coming I should have received mine own with usury.

[*Note here the Master's minimum requirement is normal growth, such as exemplified by compound interest.*]

Take therefore the talent from him, and give it unto him which hath ten talents. For unto every one that hath shall be given, and he shall have more abundance: but from him that hath not shall be taken away even that which he hath.

And cast ye the unprofitable servant into outer darkness: there shall be weeping and gnashing of teeth. (*Matt. 25:14-29*)

In this homely illustration of the Law of Natural Selection, Jesus taught that man has a simple choice of growth or misery. Nor was evolution a new teaching from Jesus. Prince Siddhartha, called Lord Buddha, taught it fully 400 years earlier. And Krishna, Lord of the Bhagavad Gita, taught it almost before the dawn of time.

Amazingly enough we find that science and religion do agree:

The Power that created and sustains the universe works through the process of evolution.

This is our first glimpse of the *purpose* of your Hidden Power. It is the continual improvement of all creation—*Evolution!*

Cooperate with Your Hidden Power

How can you cooperate with your Hidden Power to gain a better life? The answer is clear in the parable of the talents. We must work to further the evolutionary process within ourselves. In other words, we must work to build those qualities which make us strong, happy, prosperous, and wonderful and withdraw support from our weakening traits, letting them disappear back into the nothingness of their origin.

This is not a pious platitude. There are practical methods of accomplishment, with richly rewarding results. A sketchy understanding of evolution was enough to help one alcoholic. He came to realize his drinking was an escape, an attempt to drown his feeling of "being left behind by the world." By working for growth in the weaker areas of his life, he shortly eliminated his need to escape. He treated each desire for more drink as a spur to work for greater self-improvement. For the last five years he has steadily achieved successes he had never before dreamed possible.

Naming the Secret of Greatness

Let's select a name for the Secret of Greatness, the Hidden Power within you, creator and sustainer of the Universe. It is called many names by men of various beliefs—Nature, First Cause, the Unknowable, Brahma, Allah, Tao, Jehovah, the Great Spirit, the Christ Principle. A name is not too important, but we'll risk losing a few die-hard atheists and choose the simple term, God.

We asked, How can you use the Secret of Greatness within you to . . . ? Now we can rephrase the question: How can you use the God within you to bring orderly growth and happiness into your life?

Some people may be affronted at the idea of *using God*. Don't let them bother you; they are merely suffering from a lack of understanding. They use God every day, just as everyone else does. And if they would learn to use God more effectively they would be happier, healthier, and more prosperous. God is the very substance of the air you breathe, the food you eat, the house you live in, and the mind you think with. This is God in the impersonal aspect which manifests as nature, or natural law.

The wonderful part of natural law is it works the same way for everybody. If you are trying to wire a simple electric circuit to operate your doorbell, you may do it improperly a hundred times. But when you finally satisfy the laws of electricity and produce a correct circuit, the doorbell will ring. Natural laws hold no grudges; they function *every time anyone* uses them properly, and malfunction every time they are misapplied. Because they are *impersonal*, they *cannot refuse to work for you*. No matter what your desire, it can be yours if you understand the laws concerning it and *use them*. But be sure you are using them *constructively!*

The Magic That Makes
Anything Possible

How can *you* use God so much more effectively that you completely change the course of your life? There is a simple, four-step formula by which anything is possible. We will call it the Formula for Personal Creation:

1. UNDERSTAND GOD'S PURPOSE AND UNIFY WITH IT.
2. ELIMINATE ALL FEAR AND DOUBT.
3. APPLY THE GOD-POWER DIRECTLY TO THE PROBLEM AREA.
4. RELEASE IT TO GOD. RESULTS FOLLOW.

The formula itself is a statement of natural law. Therefore it cannot refuse to work for *you*. You can make it your personal Secret of Greatness!

A word of caution is in order. Don't rush off to try this thing before you know what you are doing! You wouldn't start to build a bridge before the plans were drawn; disaster could be the result. It is absolutely necessary to understand the details of each step. Let's start at the beginning.

In seeking God's purpose we are not concerned with some beautiful oriental theory of an ultimate plan which may be manifested in 25 million years. We need only be interested in that part of the Divine Plan which applies directly to this life, here and now!

How shall we look for God's immediate purpose? If you notice an unfamiliar machine and wonder what it is designed to accomplish, you can get a pretty good answer by watching it in operation. The clue to the purpose of anything is its product. So what can we learn of God's product? We have found that science and religion agree:

The Creator of the universe works through evolution.

You may complain that evolution is a process, not a product. So it is, but its duration is so great as to put the end product in the same category as the 25 million year oriental theory.

So, as practical people we can state: *God's purpose is evolution*—the growth and improvement of everything, both individually and collectively. Therefore, *God's purpose for you must be your personal evolution—Growth.*

Making the Formula Work For You

How shall you unify with God's purpose? Simply by joining it, by making it your own. This creates a set of "ground rules" for using the Formula for Personal Creation. You may use it to achieve or acquire anything that:

1. Is good for you, good for your personal growth and self-development.

2. Hurts no one, will not hinder the growth, well-being, or happiness of anyone else.

Danger! You may be able to use the formula to hurt someone else. *Don't do it!* No matter how great the wrong someone has done you, your use of these principles to "get even" will bring you punishment far beyond any vengeance imaginable. Observe the two simple ground rules at all times and be safe.

How to Unify Your Desires

If your purpose coincides with God's, your desires will partake of the Divine also. First ask yourself, "What, specifically, is my desire? Why do I want to use the formula?" It is best to write your desire on a piece of paper. This will force you to think it through. Then test it against the ground rules. As a first example, let's assume you wrote, "I want a new car."

Ground rule question 1: Is it good for you? It is always good to have nice things as long as you can care for them properly and they are not a burden.

Ground rule question 2: Does it hurt someone else? You

didn't ask to steal a car, did you? As long as you don't acquire it unfairly, it can't hurt someone else for you to get a new automobile.

Both answers are "yes," so we can consider our desire unified and compatible with God's purpose. Nature is lavish and abundant. It is generally quite proper to demonstrate God's abundance by using the formula to increase your material comforts. But don't expect the heavens to open up and deposit a new car in your driveway. The law always works, but through apparently natural channels. And again, the scope of the gift is limited by the "child's" capacity to appreciate and use it, not by the Father's capacity to give.

It isn't always so easy to answer the ground rule questions. Let's try a more complex example.

Attractive and unattached young Susie writes: "I want a date with Bob for Saturday night."

Is it good for Susie? Wholesome recreation in congenial company at the time for play is bound to be good for anyone.

Does it hurt someone else? We can't be sure of this answer. If Bob has a date with some other girl, it is dead wrong for Susie to cause him to break it. Or perhaps Bob just isn't interested. Because of the uncertainty, she gets a "no" answer to this one.

How can Susie correct this and be able to use the formula? There is only one way. She must adjust or modify her desire until it passes *both* test questions. Nothing less is acceptable!

Let's generalize Susie's desire to: "I want a date for Saturday night with a congenial and enjoyable male companion." It is all right to hope her date will be with Bob, but she must be extremely careful *not to control anyone* by using the formula.

Let's emphasize the method of unifying with God's purpose for *each use* you make of the Formula for Personal Creation:

Examine your desire and modify it until you are certain it passes the two test questions. "Good for you?" "Hurts no one?" Be honest in your appraisal! If there is the slightest doubt or uneasy feeling, don't kid yourself—your desire needs more work.

Your own subconscious mind is a gateway to all the power in the universe. It is truly your Gateway to Success. It will open wide when you have satisfied the inner self that your desires are pure and in harmony with God's purpose.

Using the Formula to Police Your Motivations

Many ideas will enter your thinking and tend to cloud the issue. Don't be confused by the many carry-overs of the orthodox morality of the mid-Victorian age. These "pseudo morals" or inhibitions are just as harmful as their opposite extremes of "free love" and the like. Resolve your doubts by going back to a simple understanding of God's purpose—evolution. Nature is God's great example of His purpose in action; look to it for your inspiration.

Another way to look at it is: you must *police your motivations!* Ask each desire in your heart why you want it. What part of God's great purpose is it trying to fulfill? Throw out anything that seems even remotely negative.

Let's take a real life example with living complexities:

A young married executive suddenly realized he had a terrific urge to have an affair with his attractive secretary. He was nervous, had trouble sleeping, and his work began to suffer.

There are two major negative aspects to this desire.

First, he made a contract in good faith to be "true" to his wife. This should not be violated. Second, sexual relations with his secretary might jeopardize his job, or at best, cost him a valuable employee. He looked at his apparently negative desire and asked it why.

All motivations stem from the general, creative, evolutionary purpose of the universe. All urges are God-given in their general sense. It is only in the particularization of desire that there is chance for human error. Behind the specific wish for an affair with his secretary lies the very natural, wholesome need for love, affection, and that wonderful expression of unity and creation, loving sex.

The particularized desire got a "no" answer to both ground rule questions. It would be bad for him to violate his marriage contract. Also, he should not attempt to control, and possibly hurt, his secretary. As the policeman of his motivation he asked his urge, "Why are you here?"

The answer came from his heart, "You are entitled to real love, tenderness, affection, and sex. As your God-given drive, I want these things for you."

Now he recognized the urge in its general or God-given state. He is entitled to the fulfillment of his drives, but as long as he is contractually bound to one woman in marriage, he must seek his love, affection, and sex at home. He turned his attention to straightening out his marriage, to rekindling the old romance. As it turned out, it was impossible to satisfy both partners; so the marriage was legally terminated, leaving each free to seek love and affection from a more suitable mate.

The lesson you should derive from this example is: behind each specific urge there lies a basic general desire which is God-given and *good*. Your particularization may be negative, but when we look at the drive behind it there is only the natural goodness of God's evolutionary purpose.

Then we are ready to make a choice. We can either (1) modify our expression of the desire until it passes both test questions, or (2) simply use the generalized, pure version of the urge as the object of our efforts, relying on Infinite Intelligence for the best specific.

Returning to our example of the young executive, he found it best to work with the general version of his desire. He did everything within reason to save his marriage, but his partner decided it was dead and "wanted out." So he could not use the formula to keep her from divorcing him.

Now Use the Magic Formula Every Day

We have cited several examples of how to work with your desires and police your motivations. Up to here it has been all talk. Now it's time for you to do something about it.

Find a quiet place where you will not be distracted. Do it today. If you don't have time, *make time!* This could be the turning point of your whole life, it is *your chance* to unify with God's purpose.

Sit quietly alone. Now summon up each of your heart's desires and study them individually. *Police your motivations.* If a specific urge puzzles you, talk to it as if it were a person. Ask it, "Why?" and the answer *will* come from your inner self.

As you bring all your desires into harmony with God's purpose, you will experience a feeling of deep inner satisfaction. Enjoy it and expand it until you are confident you have thoroughly united with the Divine Plan of evolution.

It may take an hour or a week to achieve this feeling.

Don't stop! Keep at it until you *know* it is *yours.* This completes the first step of our Formula for Personal Creation. Once accomplished it is easy to maintain, but it should be renewed for each use of the formula.

Have you achieved the feeling?

It will do little good to continue until you do. You want greater health, wealth, love, and prosperity. Work for it! You will find it fun and rewarding. Christ said: "Take my yoke upon you. . . . For my yoke is easy, and my burden is light."

You will feel light hearted and confident when you *know* you have unified with God's purpose.

How
to Live
Without Fear

> "... *perfect love casteth out fear.*"

Many people are confused by this quotation because they think hate is the opposite of love. The understanding comes when they realize that hate is just an extreme form or product of fear. Love's opposite is

chapter two

fear, and it is a powerful force because it is really *negative love.*

Trying to apply your GOD-POWER to a problem while full of fear and doubt is like operating a computer that is full of short circuits. You will get results, but no one can predict what kind. This is why the second step of our Formula for Personal Creation is: *eliminate all fear and doubt.*

Let's Eliminate All Fear and Doubt

In step one we contact the GOD-POWER by joining in Its purpose. In step two we draw It to us by removing the fears which obstruct the channel of flow. It's like getting water out of a hose. Step one is turn on the faucet. Step two is get the kinks out so the water can flow through. Fear restricts the flow of GOD-POWER into your life just as certainly as kinks restrict the flow of water in your hose.

Let's seek a better understanding of fear. Love manifests itself as willingness to give of the self, so fear must be the desire to withhold or take away the self. Both love and fear strongly attract their objects. We will illustrate with a simple give-and-take situation.

We have agreed that give is love and take is fear. If you offer a dog a bone he will be attracted to you, your love or giving being the cause. Now reverse the procedure. Snatch a bone away from a dog and he will also be attracted to you, but this time your fear or taking is the cause.

Now consider the difference in the dog's attitude toward you in the two instances. Your fear not only aroused his interest in you, it put him in a belligerent mood also. Fear always brings out the negative qualities in the objects it attracts. Similarly love is a magnet, but it brings out its objects' positive qualities.

The elimination of fear is a major accomplishment in your life, whether you choose to use the rest of our formula or not.

A life insurance salesman had three hot prospects for large policies in one day, but each bought from a competitor. Somehow the disappointment shook his confidence and he began to approach each new prospect with the fear of another refusal. For weeks he sold almost nothing. As a last resort before firing him, the sales manager gave him a pep talk and a book on the elimination of fear. He used it and went on to become the best salesman in the district.

Treat Fear as a Desire—
and Eliminate It

By recognizing fear as a desire we have gained a way to get rid of it. Step two of our formula unfolds naturally out of step one. Since it is a *desire to withhold yourself*, fear must be treated like any other desire. We must again police our motivations.

As a specific urge, *fear fails both ground rule test questions.* It is bad for you because it attracts negative experience, and it hurts the object by bringing out its negative qualities. But we know that behind each negative particularization there is a broad general desire which is God-given and good.

Behind any fear is the logical urge to have positive rather than negative experience. It is only in the specific inclination to withhold the self that human error has crept in. You are cured when you replace the fear with love. Instead of withholding yourself from the object, face it mentally and ask what you must *give* to turn it into a pleasant experience. Then, *"perfect love casteth out fear."*

A young college boy studied hard and learned his subjects, but at examination times he "blanked out." His fear of failure caused him to withdraw his mental powers just when he needed them most. A counselor explained he must *give up* his belief that examinations are a stumbling block to his education. After much discussion he began to realize that tests are simply opportunities for the student to display his new knowledge. He changed his attitude and soon began to enjoy his little opportunities. As a result, he finished in the top ten percent of his class.

How to Classify Your Fears and Defeat Them

People experience hundreds of different fears as they go through life, but all fall into one of the three chronological categories.

1. The past—fear of punishment—*guilt*.
2. The present—fear of chance—*the law of averages*.
3. The future—fear of failure—*anxiety*.

These urges to withhold the self often occur in combinations, but we will find it useful to study them individually.

Guilt Is Your Worst Enemy

Guilt is a dilemma. It is fear of punishment coupled with an equal fear you won't be punished and so must carry your remorse forever. Most of us ignore our guilts or "sweep them under the rug," but it doesn't work! They keep popping into your quiet moments saying, "You need to be punished! You deserve to be punished! Someday you *will* be punished!"

Even a little guilt can create a "living Hell." *You can free yourself.* Pay the price—it's worth it!

1. MAKE A LIST. Start preparing for freedom. Sit quietly and make a list of all your guilts. Keep asking yourself, "What am I ashamed of?" And record all your answers. You can be critically honest and objective because you aren't going to show your list to anybody. List everything that comes to mind which might reasonably invoke criticism. Several sittings over a period of two or three days is best. Make your list as comprehensive as possible.

When you feel it is complete, consider this story:

> And the scribes and Pharisees brought unto him a woman taken in adultery; and when they had sat her in the midst, they said unto him, Master, this woman was taken in adultery, in the very act. Now Moses in the law commanded us that such should be stoned: but what sayest thou? . . . But Jesus stooped down and with his finger wrote on the ground, as though he heard them not.
>
> So when they continued asking him, he lifted himself up and said unto them, He that is without sin among you, let him first cast a stone at her. And again he stooped down and wrote on the ground. And they which heard it, being convicted by their own conscience, went out one by one, beginning at the eldest, even unto the last. And Jesus was left alone, and the woman standing in the midst.
>
> When Jesus had lifted up himself and saw none but the woman, he said unto her, Woman, where are these thine accusers? Hath no man condemned thee? She said, No man, Lord. And Jesus said unto her, Neither do I condemn thee: go, and sin no more. (*John 8:3-11*)

Now look at *your* list of "sins" or guilts. Know that the Universe (or God) *does not condemn you* any more than Jesus condemned the woman taken in adultery. But if you are to be free, you must accept the commandment, *"Go, and sin no more."* A high sounding resolve is not enough, however. You must learn the lesson of each mistake so *you can avoid it* in the future.

A "sin" is just a mistake, and you are "forgiven" when you understand its cause and take positive action to prevent its recurrence.

2. MAKE GUILT A DESIRE. Take each guilt or "sin" on your list and treat it as a present desire. Examine it in the light of Step one—police your motivation and understand how you should modify the urge to meet the ground rule tests. Now you understand the true cause of the mistake. You erred in your particularization of a God-given general desire. Since you know where you went wrong you are not going to be stupid enough to make that mistake again.

Oh, yes! You may make other mistakes, but you will learn from them also. Go through this process for each entry on your list. When you have finished you are ready to attack your guilt on the second front.

A middle aged woman took two weeks to produce a thirty-seven page list of guilts. No wonder her life had seemed one calamity after the other! Then she devoted two hours a day toward working through to God for each entry. During the weeks that followed, things seemed to change their attitude towards her. The car stopped scraping her garage door, dishes stopped falling on the floor, dinners didn't burn any more, and even the neighbor's dog quit messing up her front lawn. She began to learn the meaning of "the peace that passeth all understanding," and this gave her inner strength to face up to her problems. She feels useful now, for the first time in her life.

3. SUBSTITUTE A PLUS FOR A MINUS. "Stepping out" on your husband or wife is the type of mistake where all you can do afterwards is, *"go, and sin no more."* But most mistakes require some form of restitution before they are finally erased as guilts. If you have spoken in anger and hurt someone

deeply, you should definitely apologize in person. If you have stolen or cheated you must make physical restitution; otherwise the Universe will certainly rob you of your "ill gotten gains."

However, it is quite reasonable to replace a stolen article anonymously. Suffering the embarrassment of personally returning a physical object won't help anyone. It is only necessary that the rightful owner receive what is his.

A young lady had to say, "I can't return Mary's ring, I've lost it myself." That's a direct example of the Universe robbing you of your ill gotten gains. More often your losses will not be so directly connected with the subject matter. They may manifest as accidents, unusual medical expenses, loss of a good job, or you name it.

What shall our girl do now that she has already lost Mary's ring? Make restitution anyway, to the best of her ability. Send Mary a present of equal value to the ring, but it must be done either anonymously or with a full explanation. Then in its own time and way, the Universe will make amends to all parties.

When you have made restitution for each possible entry on your list, you are ready for the final cleansing action.

4. MAKE A CLEAN SWEEP. Review your list of guilts once more. Remember the lesson of each mistake and know that you have done your best to make restitution. Now, *stop!* Are you carrying a grudge against somebody? Do you condemn someone in your heart for any action? *You have the power to forgive* all your own transgressions, but you *cannot* use it until you have first forgiven everybody else. Realize that the other fellow's sins or mistakes are no different from yours. They, too, are caused by error in specializing a God-given desire. Recognize the God-given urge behind the other's negative ac-

tion and release him by saying aloud, *"Go, and sin no more."* When you have done this for each of your fellow men, you are in position to forgive yourself.

5. FORGIVE YOURSELF. Say aloud: "On behalf of the Secret of Greatness, and with the full force of the GOD-POWER within me, I fully and freely forgive myself for all my past sins or mistakes. I forgive myself, even as I have forgiven all those whose mistakes have hurt me. I resolve to go, and sin no more."

If you have been *sincere* you will feel a strong sense of peace sweep over you. You will know you are truly forgiven because you have given of yourself. You have given understanding and restitution to others and yourself. Your giving is the "perfect love" which "casteth out fear." Your guilt is no more. *You are free!*

Making the Law of Averages Work for You

Our second category of fear is that of the unknown. It is fear of accidents or mishaps which appear to be the result of chance or the law of averages. This is not a result of your past actions, rather it is the product of pure ignorance.

What is this thing called chance? It may seem to be the unknown, but one man's chance is another's certainty. Huge business enterprises are built on this principle. Horse racing may be a gamble to the two dollar bettor, but it's a profitable business for the track. It's a matter of understanding this thing we call the *law of averages. Make it work for you: don't fight it.*

1. LEARN HOW TO FIGURE THE ODDS. The first principle of working with "chance" is: "You don't have to win them all." How long would a gambling casino stay in business

if the house won every bet? Similarly, when the New York Yankees get ten or fifteen games ahead of the league, their attendance falls off. If you expect to win everything, all the time, you are a *child*.

The adult knows he must lose *almost* as often as he wins. This doesn't bother him if he is operating the law of averages instead of being manipulated by it. You will remain a victim of chance until you put forth the effort necessary to learn the odds. A sucker "draws to an inside straight," and on that rare time he hits he will probably lose to the professional's full house.

2. Don't Accept Blind Chance. Let's make a flat statement: *there is no such thing as chance.*

It is an illusion caused by ignorance. The same circumstances that appear as chance to the uninformed are the certain operation of *law* to those who have bothered to learn it. Even physical "accidents" like automobile crashes are not caused by chance. They are attracted—often as a product of guilt.

"Hi, Cat, what's wrong with you today?" was the standard way of greeting her. "Accident prone" is what the psychologist called it. Throughout her teens she had an endless series of accidents and minor diseases. Broken finger, slashed foot, strep throat, sprained ankle, abscessed tooth, boils on the posterior, arm in a cast; the list of her maladies read like the log of an emergency hospital. Under analysis it was discovered that she had accepted the guilt for her parents' permanent separation, though she was only four years old at the time. She faced the problem and forgave her parents and herself. Then, when she started to claim divine guidance and protection as her birthright, the sickness and accidents faded into the past.

"Accidents" never happen to people who are using the law!

Take Charge of the Game

It may seem "natural" to fear the unknown, but "perfect love casteth out fear."

The desire to withhold the self from the unknown situation always attracts and magnifies negative experience. As before, you must face the issue and ask it what you should *give*. The answer comes: put forth the necessary effort to gain an understanding of everything you fear. In other words, look upon life as a poker game and decide to be a professional player. Quit being the sucker who draws to the inside straight. *Learn the odds!* Start using the law to your own advantage.

Learn to *live* life; don't just lean back and let it live you. It's like a child learning to swim. At first he is terribly afraid to put his head in the water. But he soon learns the water cannot hurt him if he understands its principles and applies them intelligently. With practice he overcomes his fear and learns to be at home in the water. Then he thoroughly enjoys it. He uses the laws of the water properly as an acquired habit, and this produces much pleasure for him. It is possible only because he has put forth the mental and physical effort to transform the unknown into the certainty of the familiar.

Most people still let life live them, so they are full of fear of the unknown. But like the swimming child, you can learn to use the laws of life properly, as an acquired habit. It will produce much pleasure for you, but only after you have transformed the unknown into the certain.

How shall you go about making this transformation? How can you grasp life by the reins and take control of it?

First understand that the entire universe functions according to natural law. The physical sciences give us some understanding of the nature of material things, psychology gives us a look at the laws of mind, and religion provides some insight into the laws of spirit. But the universe is not divided into neat little compartments. *It is one whole.* And so are *you!*

Quit thinking of yourself as a body with a mind and perhaps a soul or spirit. Become a whole being by realizing you have always been one. When you say "I am," stop thinking "I am my body." This puts you right into the category of our two dollar bettor, subject to all the rigors of chance. But when you develop the concept of yourself as a whole being, a spirit or soul expressing itself through one whole mind-body, you are set apart as an owner of the track.

You have already cleansed yourself of guilt, so you have nothing to fear from the past. Resolve that you will no longer fear the present. Apply the Formula for Personal Creation to every little corner of your life where doubt or insecurity exists. Control your life now! Where the certainty of control exists, there is no room for fear. Take "title to your race track" and *be free.*

How to Overcome Anxiety and Stop Worrying

There can be only one more kink left in your hose, only one remaining obstruction to the flow of your GOD-POWER. It is that fear of failure which manifests as worry or anxiety. These feelings cause more misery than anything else on earth, but it is all so pointless! Anticipation of failure is more degrading to a being than failure itself. Christ said of this: *"Take therefore no anxious thought for the morrow: for the morrow shall take thought for the things of itself. Sufficient unto the day is the evil thereof."* (Matt. 6:34)

Many people leave the word *anxious* out of the quotation and use it as an excuse to sit on their backsides waiting for the manna to fall from heaven. These are the "have-nots" of our society.

A better understanding is exhibited by today's enlightened businessman. Of course he *plans* for the future! He regularly forecasts his sales and cash flow, adjusts production schedules, and plans for profit maximization. But in a very real sense, he may not be sure where the money is coming from to meet next month's payroll. However, he knows he doesn't have to work with absolute physical certainties. He is using the law of averages and has faith it will work for him. Therefore he need take no anxious thought for tomorrow. He does his best today, including planning for the future. Then there is no sense in worrying about it.

Your obvious comment is: "Anybody can tell me it's pointless to worry, but who can *show* me how to stop?"

One young man of twenty-two was such a "worry wart" and so full of anxiety that he developed migraine headaches and a stomach ulcer. The doctor prescribed nerve pills and put him on a strict ulcer diet—practically nothing but cottage cheese. He felt much better for about two weeks, but then he had a relapse. The same old symptoms returned, only this time it was worse. Along with the old miseries, he also got violently ill every time he dared taste alcohol, tobacco, or meat. It was an untenable situation for that cigar smoker who considered life's greatest pleasure a Martini before his steak dinner. He sought help in the study of the laws of the mind and discovered that his doctor could only treat the symptoms. The real cure had to come from within himself. *He had to change his way of thinking!* As he successfully eliminated worry and anxiety from his habitual thought patterns, his physical symptoms subsided. It took several months to effect a complete cure, but the side benefits such as the promotion on his job proved it to be a price-less undertaking.

You can do in less than two weeks what it took that man several months to accomplish, if you will only pay the price.

Make God Your Partner

The price is your unqualified *acceptance of God as your partner* in every phase of your life. God *is* your partner, whether you like it or not. But you will suffer from worry and anxiety until you *realize* and *accept* it. This must take place deep within your being; you can't give it mere intellectual lip service and expect results. It must be a vital part of *you!*

How shall you *experience* this partnership with God? Let's try a sneaky answer. *You already have*—if you have properly completed step one of the Formula for Personal Creation. If you have examined and modified your desires, policed your motivations, and experienced the knowledge that your wishes and dreams are all compatible with God's purpose, then you have only to let the light dawn. You have made God's purpose your own. So when two people join together in a common purpose, aren't they called partners? In step one, by joining God, you experience the feeling that God has joined you. Keep that feeling alive as you go about your daily tasks. Keep thinking, "God *is* my partner." Whenever worry or anxiety tries to intrude, ask it, "If God is for me, who can be against me?"

Some worries have lived with you a long time and are firmly entrenched. But that's no excuse to harbor them any longer! Let's say you have already asked, *"If God is for me, who can be against me?"* and you are still racked with anxiety. *This is a critical point.* It raises the question of dominance. Will you be master of your mind, or will you give up and let your thoughts run you? *You are* stronger than any old worry thought. Stop everything, now! And take charge of your mind for all time!

You have *all the power of God* working with you. Reason with yourself over and over, until it becomes a part of you: "There *is* an infinite power which created and sustains the universe. I have chosen to call it God. I know that God constantly works to improve His creation through the process of evolution, because I see it demonstrated all around me in nature. As a practical matter, I can say that God's *purpose* is evolution. This urge for improvement is general to all species and specific to all individuals. Therefore I know that God's purpose for me is my own growth. My personal experience of the benefits of growth will help to advance the entire human species. I have taken the trouble to examine all my desires and modify them in the light of God's great purpose. I know that *my purpose now coincides with God's;* therefore God is my partner. God is on my side and *nothing can defeat me!"*

Pound and pound these thoughts into your being until there is no room left for worry or anxiety. When an occasional thought challenges your partnership with God, meet it by policing your motivation for the contemplated action. To re-examine the desire and be sure it conforms to God's purpose is to master its challenge. Be constantly alert to detect and destroy each worry thought as it approaches. If you persevere, within two weeks you will realize that you are living completely without fear.

Thus you have completed the first half of step two of our Formula for Personal Creation. Step two is *eliminate all fear and doubt.*

3. Figure Out Why He Wants Your Success.

In our hose analogy we called *fear* the kinks in our GOD-POWER hose. Similarly, *doubts* are the leaks. We had to get rid of our fears because water won't flow at all through a kinked hose. Doubt isn't necessarily that big a problem; you can get lots of use out of a hose with just a few leaks in it. It is reasonable to have a little healthy skepticism until you have *successfully used* the formula. Just don't let it dampen your enthusiasm for trying!

However, one form of doubt is like a gaping hole in your hose. It will waste all the energy so that not even a trickle reaches your nozzle. It's that nasty little voice which says: "This thing won't work for me because I don't deserve it. I haven't earned it." You will never get results if you are harboring any trace of this feeling. If you can't patch this leak, you might just as well turn off the faucet and forget the whole thing.

By a detailed policing of your motivations and a new understanding of your role in the universe, you built and accepted your partnership with God. You learned the lessons of your actions, made any necessary restitution, and forgave yourself and all others for the mistakes of the past. Now you are certain the universe is not mad at you. It can no more hold a grudge than the laws of mathematics, and since it holds nothing against you, it has no reason to say "no" to your desire. You only need a reason for it to say "yes."

This brings us to that glorious promise of the Master: *"I am come that they might have life, and that they might have it more abundantly."* (John 10:10)

Jesus explained your relationship to God as that of Father and child, working as partners in evolution. Aren't even earthly fathers interested in their children's development?

This is the completed patch, the reason for the universe to say "yes." Your desire stems from your Father, God. You are asking for its fulfillment as a gift from your loving Father. Is this something for nothing? *No!* You know better, now! You deserve the gift because you are a child of God, or partner if you prefer. Any limitation is set by your capacity to use it, not by God's ability to give.

If your own child worked to understand you and your partnership in his growth and then came to ask you for a gift that would add meaning to his little life, would you refuse him? Your heart would melt, and that is your way of sensing the tremendous power such an appeal generates in the universe.

You have accepted your partnership and sonship with God. How can you doubt your Heavenly Father? Meditate on this until there is no more doubt.

Enjoy Perfect Health by Avoiding Mental Poison Pockets

The trick to working the Formula for Personal Creation consistently is to lay a groundwork of perfect confidence. Keep working with the first two steps until you know you *deserve* results.

Chapter One showed how to turn on

chapter three
▼

your GOD-POWER, Chapter Two showed how to prepare the channel. Now Chapter Three shows how to direct it to specific problems. We want to focus the GOD-POWER directly on the desire or problem area. You can't very well bring a fuzzy concept into sharp focus, so it is the purpose of Chapters Three through Twelve to help clarify your thinking in typical problem areas.

Each of us uses the GOD-POWER every second of every day, but without proper focusing we tend to achieve random or confused results. When you have learned the techniques of how to focus, your heart's desire is as easy to achieve as your daily bath. The basic tool for focusing is applied knowledge. You must understand the natural laws whose misuse cause problems or lack in your life. A clear definition of the problem and its causes is always a major contribution to the solution. We will illustrate the focusing process by turning our attention to your health.

What Psychosomatic Medicine Means to You

Modern medicine has adopted the term *psychosomatic* for an ever increasing list of diseases and disorders it recognizes as being of mental origin—that is, *caused by the mind*. We can go a step further: each of us is exposed to the virus or bacteria of dozens of diseases almost daily, but we seldom catch anything. Under the direction of the subconscious mind, your body has an amazingly effective system for eliminating the various disease-producing organisms. Only when the mind blocks the efficient functioning of your protective mechanisms is your resistance lowered and disease or disorder the result.

In this sense we can say all disorder and disease is mentally caused, either directly as in psychosomatic illness, or indirectly as sickness contracted because of a lowering of the body's natural resistance. Certainly modern medicine is good, and doctors provide much needed relief from suffering. However they must treat the physical symptoms, not the mental cause. The surgeon removes your ulcer or cancer, but unless *you* change your pattern of thinking and acting, it may return in aggravated form.

How Your Mind Can Make You Sick

Our first lesson is: *There is a mental cause behind each manifestation of disease or disorder.* No matter how good your medical doctor may be, he cannot effect a *permanent* cure until you have removed the mental cause.

Specific negative thought patterns may cause widely varying manifestations of illness in different individuals, but we can be sure that every negative pattern produces an undesirable effect. Each one is a dangerous poison pocket. We will consider the most common in table form. This table is a gross oversimplification, but it should provide a means to examine the problem.

The Six Mental Poison Pockets

MENTAL POISON	RESULT
1. Hatred, bitterness, resentment.	Boils, skin rash, blood disorders, cancer, allergies, heart trouble.
2. Confusion, frustration, anger.	Common cold, pneumonia, tuberculosis, disorders of the eyes, ears, nose, and throat.
3. Anxiety, impatience, greed.	High blood pressure, migraine headaches, ulcers, poor eyesight, impaired hearing.

4. Defeatism, pessimism, cynicism.	Low blood pressure, anemia, polio, diabetes, leprosy, low income.
5. Revulsion, fear, guilt.	Accidents, cancer, personal failure, poverty, poor sex, boils, "bad blood."
6. Antagonism, inferiority, introversion.	Allergies, headaches, lack of friends, heart murmur, accidents.

You seldom find a pattern which fits into just one pocket. Most negative thought groups are blends of poisons with a little positive stirred in to help mask them. The table is not a ready rule of thumb to determining the cause of a specific disease or disorder. It should be considered more as a poetic warning of the *danger* of harboring negativity of any kind.

AVOID POISON POCKET ONE: HATRED—BITTERNESS —RESENTMENT. In the eighth month of pregnancy a young woman was deserted by her husband. She was left alone in a big city with no relatives and not even a really close friend. Her resentment at having to accept county aid soon grew into a bitter hatred of all men, and she led a lonely, miserable life. She constantly justified her feelings with, "Anybody would hate men after what happened to me."

When she developed a series of painful boils, she cried out in anger, "How can there be a God? If there were one he would help me!"

Finally a well-meaning friend told her she was doing it to herself. She drove the friend out of her room in anger. But after another boil she was ready to listen to anything. She apologized to her friend and asked for more information. It took three books on mental healing before she realized that she must forgive her ex-husband. At long last she started to mentally send him God's love. It quickly softened her whole personality, with the result that she not only got rid of her boils, but found a wonderful new husband as well.

There is no way to be happy in this life until you release all traces of hatred, bitterness, and resentment. Wash them away in the living water of forgiveness. Forgiveness is *to give for*—to give love for bitterness. *"Vengeance is mine, saith the Lord."* Let the universe worry about punishing the wrongdoer. You forgive him! You can't afford the harm to yourself which comes from withholding forgiveness.

One of the great wonders of life is the fact it is never too late to be happy. You may have wallowed in bitterness and resentment for years, but you can forgive and start to enjoy life, *now!*

A salesman quit a good job because he thought he was being cheated on his commissions. He became so bitter he couldn't hold another job. He went downhill for three years before his wife put a stop to it. She told him she was leaving him if he didn't immediately change his attitude toward employers. Reluctantly, he sat down to work on forgiveness. He finally realized his former boss might have been honest after all, and this made him feel a lot better. With this new attitude he again set out job hunting. He swallowed his pride and asked his old boss for another chance. In six months he was more successful than he had ever been.

Avoid Poison Pocket Two: Confusion—Frustration—Anger. The president of a small corporation was having business troubles which began to affect his health. An interesting pattern developed. Each month he spent several days in bed with a fever, right after seeing his profit and loss statement. For nearly a year the business and his health got progressively worse. During a month long bout with pneumonia he saw the pattern and decided to grow up. He told himself there is room for only one emotion in the business world, and that is *enthusiasm*. Attacking his problems with new insight and vigor, he straightened out the business. He hasn't had a fever in years.

Confusion, frustration, and anger are symptoms of emotional immaturity. They tend to be characteristic of children. Part of growing up is learning to tolerate the ambiguous or uncertain for the time it takes to understand it. We discussed putting forth the effort to learn the odds and change the unknown into the certainty of the familiar. Confusion and frustration are the result of your failure to give that effort. But if you really let it "get your goat," you still belong in diapers. You can't afford to stay an emotional child. *Grow up!*

AVOID POISON POCKET THREE: ANXIETY—IMPATIENCE—GREED. Anxiety, impatience and greed fill the third poison pocket. These are products of insecurity and the terrible illusion of separation from God. You are automatically healed when you increase your experience of *Partnership with God.* (Chapter Two again.)

A young housewife was unduly anxious to show her mother-in-law she was a good housekeeper. Several minor oversights in dusting that she noticed at crucial moments made her even more impatient with herself, and she began to develop severe migraine headaches whenever her mother-in-law visited. A simple explanation of her partnership with God was the beginning of the cure. She decided her mother-in-law was also God's partner and only needed to be treated as such. Gradually she stopped being anxious to make an impression and grew to accept her husband's mother as a friend. Now there isn't a migraine between them.

This brings us to the most degrading member of the trio, greed. Have you ever noticed the small group of little old ladies who almost claw their way to the front of the line at a church "pot luck dinner"? It's a pathetic example of how greed robs even old age of its dignity. This grasping, clawing attitude of "give me mine first and most" can only bring misery. There is some of it in each of us. We must root it out. Destroy it! Replace it with the feeling of certainty that the GOD-POWER will provide for your every need.

AVOID POISON POCKET FOUR: DEFEATISM—PESSIMISM—CYNICISM. We might call this fourth poison pocket misery row since it contains defeatism, pessimism, and cynicism. These thought patterns belong to people who are already dead but don't quite have guts enough to lie down. I once knew a "professional cynic" who had developed the art to a fine point. He thought it was really funny to find something bad in the most altruistic act you could imagine. Fortunately a girl friend gave him a good look at what he was doing. He was turning into a living example of misery. His morbid cynicism had created an unpleasant atmosphere about him, and his former friends were beginning to avoid him. She showed him it is a perverted form of humor and that he couldn't afford its terrible effect on his life. He stopped in time to regain his old happiness and renew his strained friendships.

The defeatist says, "Don't try, you can't possibly succeed."

The pessimist says, "The odds are against it. The cards are stacked. Why bother to try?"

The cynic says, "Go ahead, stupid, try it. But even if you do succeed, some jackass will steal it from you."

These are all degrees of the same disease, Self-pity. Stop feeling sorry for yourself over your little defeats. Victory belongs to the man who gets up one more time than he is knocked down! Get up off that deathbed and look ahead with confidence in your own GOD-POWER. Success is yours for the *acting!*

AVOID POISON POCKET FIVE: REVULSION—FEAR—GUILT. We are told that at the beginning God looked upon His world and pronounced it *good*. Everything in creation is *good* and has its place. Your esthetic sense may occasionally be disturbed by something out of place, but that's no excuse for a feeling of revulsion. If there is no apparent good for you in something, avoid it, of course! But don't condemn anything or anybody.

Consider this ancient example of pointing the finger: Point your index finger at something as if to indicate its shame. Now while you are pointing, look carefully at the rest of your hand. Do you see the *three* other fingers pointing back at you? To accuse someone else is to accuse yourself *threefold*.

The philosopher, Hermes, put it as: "Beauty is in the eye of the beholder." So where is ugliness? Promise yourself you will never call God's creation revolting again.

AVOID POISON POCKET SIX: ANTAGONISM—INFERIORITY—INTROVERSION. A man is beaten on the field of logic, so he becomes antagonistic and wants to fight rather than admit he is wrong. This is sheer stupidity! It's a poor cover-up for feelings of inferiority. But what is inferiority?

Do you sometimes feel inferior? Inferior to what? You are something less than all of the Infinite, so you might say you are inferior to God. But as part of God, *as an undivided part of the Infinite,* you can be no more or less important than any other part. *You are not inferior or superior to anything!* Just be glad you are a part of God, and know that your own GOD-POWER is infinite. It is second to none!

Introversion fits in this group because it is another manifestation of inferiority. The die-hard introvert will say, "No, that isn't true! I just happen to prefer my own company."

Little one, a drop that has separated itself from the ocean is just a drop, but in its proper place it is part of the great whole. It is the ocean that gives meaning and greatness to its every drop. Man is a social animal. He was planned that way. A person who rejects mankind and lives only for himself loses his own meaning. If you are not satisfied with mankind as it is, work to improve yourself and all men in the process. Service, not rejection, should be your gift to the world. It will help you to a better and better life.

How to Eliminate the Poison Pockets from Your Life

How do the poison pockets of negative thought create the terrible manifestations we have attributed to them? By their effect on your part of the GOD-POWER. In Chapter One we learned to *consciously* contact the GOD-POWER, but we are *always in unconscious contact* with it. Thus we unconsciously use the Formula for Personal Creation to attract to us the circumstances and situations which conform to our dominant thoughts.

If we are to improve our lot on this earth, we must learn to satisfy both sides of the law. It is necessary to consciously use the GOD-POWER to bring good into your life, but it is equally important to stop using it to bring misery and disease along with the good. Since you are using *impersonal* law, you have the power of choice as to how it shall be applied. The same electricity will kill a man or light a city, just depending upon how it's used. It's time to stop electrocuting yourself and start lighting up the city of your life. Work to eliminate all your negative thought patterns and thus remove the mental causes of disease and misery.

How to Heal Yourself

You must work positively to heal your present disorders and keep your mind and body in radiant, perfect health. Understand and believe that the average medical doctor is a dedicated man who would rather see you healthy and happy than earn a big fee by treating you for an illness. It is good common sense to seek competent medical help when you need it. The doctor will relieve your physical symptoms, but remember, only *you* can remove the mental causes.

When he was thirteen years old, a boy we will call Johnny, was stricken with polio. It left him with a terribly withered right leg, but somehow nature seemed to compensate by giving him added determination. Johnny had dreamed of being a football star, but now that was out of the question. He looked for another sport in which he might compete and found his high school gym team. In the rope climb and even the rings, he found his withered leg was not a handicap and managed to lead the team in these events for three straight years. He walked slowly, hitching his right leg along; but when the gun sounded start, he went hand over hand up the rope with the best in the league.

Toward the end of his last year in high school, a group of his friends decided to visit a spiritualist meeting as a lark, and asked Johnny to come along. It turned out to be much more than a lark for Johnny. The lecture was on the healing of the so-called incurable diseases. He stayed after the service to ask if the minister thought his leg could be made whole.

They embarked on a joint effort of daily prayer and weekly "laying on of hands," seeking wholeness for his maimed body. Aside from his regular morning and evening prayers, Johnny was assigned an affirmation to use throughout the day:

"The GOD-POWER within me created my body and can rebuild it. The strength is returning to my right leg, and I am being made whole, now!"

The same determination that led to success on the gym team paid off again. Progress was painfully slow at first, but Johnny held on. He never missed a prayer or a healing session, and he filled every spare moment with the affirmation. "The GOD-POWER within me created my body and can rebuild it. The strength is returning to my right leg, and I am being made whole, now!" In six months there was some obvious improvement. The hitch in his walk was being reduced to a decided limp—and his right leg was growing! It took another year to complete the healing, but Johnny never faltered. He crowded out each doubt and fear with the affirmation and left no room for any kind of negativity. Now his leg is whole, but more important, his faith is strong enough to surmount any obstacle.

There is no such thing as an "incurable" disease or condition. *Since all disease is mentally caused it can be mentally healed.* Over the years we have been taught that some diseases are harder to cure than others, and it has been done to us as we believed. However, the Master of two thousand years ago healed "incurable" diseases and said of his accomplishments, *"These works that I do shall ye do also, and even greater works shall ye do. . . ."* Shall we doubt the word of one whose dedication was so great He laid down his life to teach the power of the God-Mind within each of us?

There is a very positive value to sickness and disease. It

is an alarm system, a warning when something is wrong with a basic thought pattern. It warns you to change your way of thinking. And if you do, the alarm is turned off—you are healed. But if you persist in negative thinking, the sickness will destroy the physcial body (bring death) rather than let you do permanent damage to your Real or Immortal self. God will protect the *Real You* in spite of yourself.

How to Achieve the Secret of Perfect Health

Let's set out to specifically improve your health. First: if you feel sick, go to a doctor for treatment of your physical symptoms. The relief the doctor gives you is *good!* Be thankful for the wonderful progress our medical profession has made. Many "incurable" diseases of the past have been conquered by the steady advance of our tireless physicians.

Next: lead a sensible life. Eat a well balanced diet, get a reasonable amount of sleep, be temperate in your use of alcohol and tobacco, get enough good sex but don't kill yourself at it, use vitamins and "health foods" if they seem to help you, and learn to enjoy the time you spend working for a living. These are the normal things any reasonable person would do. They are good, but they are not quite enough!

The secret of perfect health lies in your mind, in your ability to constructively use the GOD-POWER within you.

Regain Your Unconscious Ability

Again we turn to nature. If you cut a "leg" off a starfish it will grow back! Many of the "lower" animals grow replacements for lost or damaged parts of their bodies. Wouldn't it be nice to be as smart as a starfish so you could grow a new leg if you needed it? Isn't it reasonable to assume that the same

Power which grows a new leg for the starfish could do it for you, if you would only learn to cooperate with it?

Somewhere along the ladder of evolution, man and the "higher" animals lost the unconscious ability to grow replacements for major items of their anatomy. But who can say man hasn't gained the ability to accomplish the same result by *consciously cooperating* with the vital life force, by doing with his conscious mind that which the starfish does because he doesn't know any better? We all grow new fingernails and hair and two sets of teeth, but we generally stop there. Why? Because we are taught from birth that we can go no further.

It *is* a scientific fact that the body does not replace major parts and organs *as a normal function of the unconscious healing process*. But this is simply an example of the old truism, "nature unaided fails." It's like saying a piece of iron will sink when you throw it into the water. It will, too, unless you are smart enough to make a ship out of it. We fail to grow new limbs and organs only because we are ignorant of the natural laws involved.

Using Your "Miracle" Power

The GOD-POWER within you is available to perform any sort of healing "miracle." *It will produce for you* when you learn to cooperate with it, both mentally and physically. It is infinite! It can grow a new leg, kidney, or eye as easily as it heals a scratch on your finger. The difference is not in your GOD-POWER; it's in your mind. You believe you are entitled to heal a scratch on your finger, but not to grow a new arm or gall bladder. So you don't even bother to try! But you can learn how to do it consistently for yourself and others. Either way you are proving the truth of the Master's words, *"According to your belief is it done unto you."*

So-called healing "miracles" take place regularly all over the world. Occasionally your daily newspaper carries the story of a spectacular healing at one of the major shrines, such as Lourdes. And in every large country, publications dedicated to parapsychology or psychic research carry new accounts of "miraculous healings" every month. But in general, these "miracles" only happen to people who believe them possible and go out looking for a healing. And the relief is permanent only for those who thoroughly eradicate the mental cause at the same time.

Naturally, if you are one of the physically handicapped you should make the best possible mental and social adjustment to that present fact. But here is a thought to ponder: If you are "stubborn" enough and learn to cooperate with your GOD-POWER, *you can be healed*. Some healings are spectacular and almost instantaneous; others take much time, application, and prayer. Unless you *try*, there will be no results at all!

The Law of Thought
Manifestation

Let's reduce this line of thinking to a simple law. In physics we are taught: "For every action there is a reaction." The law of Hermes is: "As above, so below." By combining these we get an extremely useful one:

For every *thought pattern* there is a comparable *physical manifestation*.

Wrong use of this law hurts us. We ignorantly harbor negative thoughts until they become patterns and manifest themselves as physical, financial, or social problems in our daily lives.

A conscientious construction worker was frequently

asked to put in overtime. His wife's loneliness quickly turned to suspicion, and she began to accuse him of "stepping out on her." The pattern became so pronounced he dreaded going home after every extra stint. One such night he stopped for a beer to prepare for the nagging. Without noticing, he sat next to a girl at the bar. A conversation developed and he wound up at her apartment, thinking, "I might as well, I'll be accused of it anyway."

Many marriages end right there, but this man loved his wife enough to try for a solution. He got her to a counselor and honestly told his story, apologizing for his action and explaining his dread of the nagging. After many tears, the wife agreed to replace the thought, "He's stepping out on me," with "It's so nice he's willing and able to make some extra money for us." Both resolved to honestly work for greater mutual consideration and understanding. They recently celebrated a happy silver wedding anniversary.

How to Use the Law

Inherent in the same law is your key to freedom. It is the straightforward way to steadily improve your health, wealth, and over-all well-being. The Apostle Paul poetically described its use with these words:

> Whatsoever things are true, whatsoever things are honest, whatsoever things are just, whatsoever things are pure, whatsoever things are lovely, whatsoever things are of good report; if there be any virtue, and if there be any praise, think on these things. (Phil. 4:8)

By positive use of the law you can cure an "incurable" disease or grow a new leg, just as certainly as you unconsciously heal a scratch on your finger. You use the same *Prin-*

ciple and *Power* in either case. *It works every time you call on it!* The technique is presented in our Formula for Personal Creation. We will illustrate the whole process now.

The secret of success is in the groundwork you build in these first two steps. In Chapter One we learned that God's purpose is your personal good, your growth and evolution. Police your motivations until you *feel* your oneness of purpose with the GOD-POWER. Carry the feeling into step two.

Using the work of Chapter Two, eliminate your fears and doubts. While you are cleaning your mental house, look back at our Six Mental Poison Pockets and get rid of any lurking mental causes by the same method. When you complete step two you have eliminated the mental cause of the very condition you wish to heal.

Next to guilt and fear, the biggest stumbling blocks are hatred, bitterness, and resentment. In our work with guilt we learned that you must forgive other's mistakes before you can forgive your own. This is the meaning of the key condition of the Lord's Prayer: "Forgive us our trespasses as we forgive those who trespass against us."

If you feel someone has wronged you so terribly that you cannot forgive him (or her), then gift wrap this book, mail it to a friend, and go on about your business. Without true forgiveness of all who have ever "wronged" you, you will never be able to use your GOD-POWER effectively. But you don't have to be silly about it either. So you forgive somebody! You aren't obliged to let him hurt you again. If a person has a strong tendency to steal, it won't help him, or you, to give him a chance at your family fortune. This teaching is not for jellyfish; it is for man. You are intelligent enough to forgive from strength, not weakness. It's all right to "carry a big stick" as long as it's meant for defense.

Apply the God-Power Directly

As you eliminate all forms of negative thought, you are completing the first part of step three along with step two. Attack each lingering bit of fear, anxiety, or negativity with the same weapon. Think to yourself—*know*—God's purpose is your perfect health, growth, evolution. You have made your peace with the universe and all its inhabitants. Because you have joined forces with Him, God must be on your side. And, "If God is for me, who can be against me?" When you *feel* this with your whole being, your spoken word becomes the law of the universe.

Apply the GOD-POWER by speaking your order to the cosmos. When you speak from this feeling of oneness, it is God speaking through you. And when God commands, the universe must obey! Say aloud:

"In the name of the Secret of Greatness, the GOD-POWER within me, I *decree* that all the energy of the universe is concentrated upon the healing of my _____ (insert your need). I am growing a *perfect body, now!* I *know* I am being completely healed."

Repeat it again and again, until you *feel in your heart* it is so.

Release It to God— Results Follow

Release it with thanks to the Infinite. It must manifest! Use the words of the Master, *"Father, I thank thee that thou hast heard me, and I know that thou hearest me always."*

According to your belief is it done unto you. If you have done your mental work, *it shall be yours!*

Don't be afraid to go back to the doctor. If he doesn't

see the improvement in your condition, you haven't achieved enough of the *feeling of oneness with God.* No healing job is too hard for the creative power of the universe. It will accomplish whatever you need. If you send your broken cigarette lighter or fountain pen back to the factory you expect results. God's results are even more certain. Do your mental work, speak your word as the law of the universe, and release it to God. Healing is yours now! Enjoy your perfect health.

▲

Increase Your
Wealth with the
Seven Magnets to Riches

Money has been
the whipping boy of the
"moralist" for centuries.
The subject of "earning
a living" is clouded with
stagnant, decaying ideas.
It's time to clear your
mind of these useless concepts and make room for
a fresh approach.

Admit it! If you

chapter four

▼

don't have more money than you need, *it's your own fault.* A little honest hindsight invariably shows that with fewer foolish mistakes *on your part,* you could already be well off financially. Just a few dollars invested in the right stock at the right time has made some men fortunes, why not you? *You have been your own worst enemy!*

Though your present station in life be panhandler or president of a major corporation, *you are there by your deliberate choice.* It may have been made because you thought you could do no better, but it was *your choice.*

Stop Blaming Others

Stop blaming circumstances, lack of education, your age, or bad breaks. As long as you feel the cause is something outside yourself, you are beaten. An emotional child may scream: "If it weren't for that dirty swindling partner of mine"—or, "If it weren't for my rotten ex-wife"—or, "The stock market crash—."

Let the little children point their fingers at the blame. An adult can see the *three* fingers pointing back at each one who would shift it.

The reward for accepting the blame for your present situation is the power to change it. Because it resulted from your choice, you must have the *power to choose something better.* This is the way to overcome all your troubles! *You can choose a more abundant life* and use the GOD-POWER to obtain it. But we have many dead ideas to eliminate before we can focus directly on the problem.

Man is a whole being; he doesn't exist in isolated compartments. Anything that hurts one part of a man detracts from his over-all well-being. The Six Mental Poison Pockets of our previous chapter will decrease your financial abundance as surely as they injure your physical health. Clean them out! As you gain more radiant health and zest for life you are moving toward material success as well.

The Seven Magnets to Riches

Let's continue the mental housecleaning. There's more than gold in your mind, if you will only look for it. Set up a program of replacing old negative concepts of money and business with positive thought patterns which will attract abundance. Unfold your seven magnets to riches. They are:

1. Speak well of money.
2. Appreciate modern business.
3. Rejoice in the wealth of others.
4. Be a team player.
5. Give value for value.
6. Pay your debts.
7. Build positive thought patterns.

1. SPEAK WELL OF MONEY. A man in tattered clothes at the bar says, "Money is the root of all evil." His seedy companion corrects him, "No! Love of money is the root of all evil."

Turn your back on both and walk away, *fast*. That is the biggest bunch of sour grapes ever heaped upon the world. You will never hear a rich man say it!

Once upon a time a Man multiplied the loaves and fishes to feed the multitudes, turned water into fine wine, healed the sick, and produced gold coins in the mouth of a fish to pay His friends' taxes. People will try to tell you this Jesus of Nazareth was a poor man. Utter nonsense! He was richer, both materially and spiritually, than any man on earth. The Master didn't carry large sums of cash because He didn't need to. If you have millions of dollars in the bank you don't have to carry other millions in your pocket. That's what checks are for. Jesus carried an unlimited supply of spiritual blank checks which He could cash at will to satisfy any material or spiritual need. He needed cash money like a hole in the head! Don't let anyone tell you He wasn't the richest man in the world.

Get away from the terrible idea that money is evil. Say over and over again, money is good. *Money is good.* It is an idea in the mind of God, a symbol of God's loving opulence, and a very practical medium of exchange. It matters not whether it takes the form of gold, currency, bank deposits, beads, bones, cattle, real estate, or acorns. Money is necessary and it is *good*. To curse it is to drive it away from you; to praise it is to attract it. Use your magnet. Praise money always.

2. APPRECIATE MODERN BUSINESS. A very able business man became Secretary of Defense under President Eisenhower. He was severely criticized for his widely quoted statement to the effect that what's good for General Motors is good for the country. Perhaps because of the political-social climate of the times, the statement was in poor taste. But whether in good taste or not, that kind of statement was and is *true*. It is necessary to look behind the furor that was raised and understand what the gentleman was trying to convey.

The strength of our country to feed, or if necessary, to fight the world lies in that method of practical organization loosely referred to as our economic system. It is a composite whole, made up of widely different parts. It includes labor unions, independent workers, farmers, engineers, small and large investors, small businessmen, professional managers, corporations, stockbrokers, bankers and many others. Each is important in his own special way to the smooth and efficient functioning of the whole. Anything that strengthens one segment of the economy without correspondingly weakening any other, must be of benefit to the whole. Therefore what's good for General Motors (and doesn't hurt anyone else) *is good* for the country.

Mr. Charlie Wilson was nearly chopped to ribbons by a bunch of people who were either too ignorant to understand or too politically biased to want to. It's easy to criticize a man, but how many of his critics could have come close to filling his shoes?

An ardent student of religion and the occult sciences had learned much about spirituality, but he made the mistake of refusing to recognize God in the business world. In effect he called God a "crook," because he went around saying all business men are "crooks" and business is designed to keep the working man down. He talked and acted this way on the job with the direct result that he was chronically unemployed. When he did find work it seemed to be always for the minimum wage. His family lived in want and had no hope for the future, not even a scrap of life insurance. He was killed in an accident at the age of 42, leaving his family to the welfare rolls.

Take a long, searching look at your own opinions of our economic system. If you want to get ahead, now is the time to recognize that modern business is good, and businessmen work for a living like everybody else. The function of private ownership—risk capital—is still the most effective way to insure economic growth and increasing plenty for all. Don't argue with success. Join it! Business built this country and is building a better material life for all, every day. Give a little more understanding next time someone says something like, what's good for General Motors is good for the country. Don't join the wolves who try to tear him apart. He may be one hundred percent right!

3. REJOICE IN THE WEALTH OF OTHERS. You often hear someone say, "I wish I had his money." But what does it really mean? "I wish I had his money because I'm afraid I'm not good enough to make it on my own." Jealousy is a manifestation of feelings of inferiority. It operates as a powerful negative magnet, repelling its object with great force. To harbor jealousy is to deny the GOD-POWER within yourself.

"Bring ye all the tithes into the storehouse, that there may be meat in my house, and prove me now herewith, saith the Lord of Hosts, if I will not open you the windows of heaven, and pour you out a blessing that there shall not be room enough to receive it." (Mal. 3:10)

The tithes are your attention and study of the laws of life, that there may be the meat of understanding in the Lord's house, your mind and heart. For this the GOD-POWER promises you abundance beyond your wildest dreams. Why should you be jealous of somebody else's wealth?

Another's Wealth Is Proof the Law Will Work For You

When you see a man of great wealth, rejoice in his good fortune. He is a living example of the fulfillment of God's promise of material blessings. If you feel you are smarter than he, all the better. You see the law working for him, make it work for you also. "Superior intelligence" is a terrific drawback until you forget, in the white heat of enthusiasm, to apply it practically. Intelligence, no matter how great, remains a side show curiosity until it accomplishes something practical.

Carry your tithe of *applied* intelligence into daily life,

that there may be the meat of understanding in the Lord's house. Then the windows of Heaven *will open up* and shower you with opulence!

Meanwhile, rejoice in the success of others. They may have acquired their opulence by accidentally working the law. So what! Let them enjoy it. They could lose theirs someday. But when you have achieved your abundance by consciously using the law, *you can have it forever!*

4. BE A TEAM PLAYER. Common to all major civilizations is some ideal like the Golden Rule. In this country it is stated, "Do unto others as you would have them do unto you." Don't make the mistake of calling this a bunch of high-sounding foolishness. The word *rule* means just what it says. It is a *law* of the universe.

A Hindu might express it, "As you do unto others, the universe will do unto you." Jesus put it, *"And with what measure ye mete, it shall be measured to you again."* (Matt. 7:2)

A junior executive moved up the ladder with great speed. In three years he "torpedoed" three successive bosses and each time he was asked to fill the vacancy. The fourth boss was older and experienced in the ways of the world. In about six months the junior again laid plans to get his supervisor's job. But this old trout smelled the pattern and baited a little trap of his own. Our climbing friend bit and was fired for misconduct. It isn't always that direct, but you can be certain the world will exact its price sooner or later.

If you want another man's job there is a wonderful way to get it. Get him a promotion! Sell his strong points sincerely at every reasonable opportunity. If your man gets promoted and you still don't get the job, *don't be bitter.* Help promote his successor! This attitude *must pay off.* And besides, it's quite comfortable. You can be honest about it. You can even tell him, "Boss, I want your job. So I'm going to do everything possible to help you get promoted."

Then live it! Loyalty of this kind cannot go unrewarded for long, but it doesn't have to work out exactly as you expect. An unusual opportunity may arise for you in another firm, or you might discover a new talent which reshapes your whole career.

Remain aloof from petty office politics and keep selling your boss' strong points. The reward of self-respect will open doors you didn't know existed. Don't sell this simple idea short. It works! It will bring you more money, respect, position, and comfort.

5. GIVE VALUE FOR VALUE. "The world owes me a living" attitude keeps its holders from advancing. Anyone who wants more than a bare subsistence income must earn it. Drop the "what's in it for me" approach and replace it with a positive, "how can I be of greater service?" You will automatically find yourself in demand for better and better positions.

It's all right to ask for a raise, but before you do, ask yourself how you can increase your usefulness to the company. If you demonstrate your increased value first you probably won't have to *ask*. Business is like football; it pays off for points on the scoreboard. If you want more money, *produce!*

Because man has learned to use some natural laws, many things are done for him that he formerly did for himself. Forklifts and conveyor belts load trucks where muscles and sweat once struggled, but nobody calls that something for nothing. It is the "profit" from intelligent use of natural law.

Your life will become more meaningful and comfortable when you take the trouble to build mental forklifts and conveyors. Learn the laws of your mind and *apply them*. They are more effective than all the machinery ever built.

6. PAY YOUR DEBTS. You probably know a few people who are actually pained at the thought of paying their debts. They concoct elaborate schemes for avoiding bill collectors and spend much time and effort figuring out new ways to buy on credit. The same effort spent in intelligently planning their financial future would bring them real prosperity.

Most of us are not that bad, but we have some of those tendencies. The old car needs new tires or a ring job, so we buy a new one and then complain about the payments for years. We must outgrow all this. The wise adult enjoys paying his bills. He gets a real feeling of satisfaction from meeting all of his obligations as they come due. He has developed the concept of the "Divine surplus," so ordering his spending that there is a cushion left out of each paycheck. By intelligent planning and self-discipline, he lives a well ordered, satisfying financial life.

Resolve to finish your growing-up process in relation to money, now. Paying your bills can be fun. Don't be a "dead beat," a "tightwad," or a "spendthrift"; live happily in the middle. Develop that concept of a Divine surplus, not for a rainy day, but to make *now* more comfortable.

7. BUILD POSITIVE THOUGHT PATTERNS. The habit of the positive approach to routine living gives us strength to handle the petty annoyances we may have felt in the past. Check your honest reaction to flies, ants, neighbor children, relatives, competitors, people of different skin color or religious faith, gophers, crab grass, the neighbor's dog, the other political party, governmental "red tape," or your spouse's habit of eating potato chips in bed.

If any one of these can "get your goat" you are still harboring thought patterns which are as dangerous as polio virus or a mad dog. They are apt to bring sickness to your pocketbook, your body, or both.

Learn to live and let live. It's not just a trite phrase. It is a necessity to comfortable, prosperous living. It may seem a big order to change your attitude toward little things, but it's worth the effort. If you want prosperity and happiness you must *work at it*.

You can make much progress with a small amount of added tolerance. The effect on *you* is quite different when you discover you are killing ants to be sanitary, not because you hate them. The good feeling that comes from such an accomplishment is beyond description, and because it increases your feeling of peace with the universe, it will find ways to increase your material abundance.

One man had no problems with ants, but flies were another story. A fly crawling on his bare skin sent him into fits of rage. His cure began when he learned that most flies prefer to live out of doors. The poor creatures are confused by the intricacies of a modern house and definitely need help to find their way out. Each time a fly annoyed him, he lovingly and patiently directed it out through the nearest door. The reward for his pains is the pleasure of a fly-free house, and the comfort of a conscience which is happy that he no longer kills in rage —not even flies. His house smells better, too, without the odor of fly sprays.

You can learn to replace irritation and rage with tolerance and understanding. When you put forth the effort to understand and resolve each potentially irritating situation, life will be peaceful, serene, enjoyable, and profitable.

This concludes our mental magnetizing for the abundant life. Obviously you can't be expected to accomplish all we have suggested in one night or one week, but that is no excuse not to start *now*. Continue your mental work until the new positive ideas become *part of your being*. Let them drive out all their negative counterparts. Diligence will be rewarded!

How great is the reward? It is whatever you ask it to be. A young accountant used the principles we are about to discuss to increase his salary from $500 per month to $2,100 per month in just over three years—without changing employers! It was hard work for him because he hadn't first done his mental magnetizing. He used the positive techniques of the Formula, but there was so much static from his old thought patterns that it greatly retarded his progress. He could have gone farther, much faster—but many would be overjoyed to do as well.

You will make progress whenever you use positive techniques. But only when your mind is magnetized can your GOD-POWER create with full effectiveness.

Let the Money Flow

We bring this subject to a close with one very significant idea. A pool of water with no outlet will become stagnant and unfit for use. Money is a dynamic, not a static commodity. In our water analogy we see that circulation is necessary to maintain its usefulness, and balancing the inflow and outflow is much more important than the size of the reservoir. Live within your means of course, but never be afraid to spend money. That's all it's good for. Always release your money with joy to do its work.

In this respect, *giving* is most important. In the example of our accountant who increased his monthly salary from $500 to $2,100 it is significant to note that his church contributions increased from $1 to $50 per week during the same period.

Further, the increases in giving were spontaneous and always seemed to precede major increases in salary.

Obviously your church or favorite charity needs the money, but there is a much more important reason for your giving. You *need* to give—not till it hurts, but definitely till it feels good—in order to keep open the channels of income and fertilize your fields of good.

Wealth beyond your fondest dreams is yours *if* you sincerely apply yourself to these principles.

▲

How to
Develop Personal
Electromagnetism

If you have enthu-
siastically started the work
of the first four chapters,
you should be noticing
some concrete improve-
ments in your life. You
should be happier, cheer-
ful, and more serene.
Your body should be full
of vitality, and you should
be developing the calm

chapter five
▼

confidence of one who is *in control of his life* and *knows it*. If you haven't sensed this yet, *now* is the time to seize control.

Carefully review each section of the work until you *really feel* the GOD-POWER surging within your being, until you *know* it is working for and through you. Feel yourself being freed from worry and fear, and becoming healthier and more prosperous. Realize your ever-growing sense of well-being.

Why Balanced Growth
Is Essential

Our purpose now is to intensify your livingness by increasing your ability to enjoy people, to deal successfully with all types in all areas of your daily life. We have agreed that our purpose in life is growth—personal evolution. Each chapter of this book has been designed to stimulate growth in some area of *your* life. However, it is important to understand that *balanced* growth is the essence of a happy existence.

If your left leg should grow a foot longer than your right, you would be pretty uncomfortable. So it is with any area of your life. If it grows too big, or if it is left behind by the growth of the rest of the organism, it will be a trouble spot until balance is restored.

How to Direct Your Growth

We are approaching the process of your growth in an orderly manner, touching each important phase of life as we go. But you are a unique individual. No other person in the world has exactly the same set of strengths and weaknesses as yours. Some are healthy but "broke," others have plenty of money but ulcers or the like, still others may have good health and plenty of money but feel that "everybody hates me." You provide your own emphasis as you work with these principles.

Only *you* can provide the direction! And it may seem like hard work. You must concentrate your efforts on the specific improvement of your weaker areas. It is only by strengthening your weak spots that you build a firm foundation for the further progress of your whole being. Don't shirk this responsibility to yourself.

The general area called human relations is a weakness for many. We will approach this by asking: How can I develop a dynamic personality, one that will attract people to me?

The answer begins with mental magnetizing. These are the Seven Steps to an Irresistible Personality:

1. Hide your bad moods.
2. Consider the feelings of others.
3. Spread cheer and optimism.
4. But don't be a "Pollyanna."
5. Keep your troubles to yourself.
6. Avoid gossip.
7. Be yourself.

You are an accomplished mental magnetizer by now, so we won't have to spend much time on these.

1. HIDE YOUR BAD MOODS. Have you ever noticed how children love to annoy the neighborhood grouch? Nobody likes to be around one unless it is to torment him. If you are a habitual grouch you are poisoning yourself. The misery you bring to others is nothing compared to what you are heaping upon yourself. *Cut it out!* You can't afford it.

But what about you usually congenial people who sometimes "get up on the wrong side of the bed"? If you wake up feeling grouchy, promise yourself *right then* you will keep your big mouth shut until you're sure something nice will come out of it. We all have occasional bad days. They get better if we are quiet, but what a mess they can become if we turn loose our venom!

There is only one course of action. If you are too grumpy to be nice, *shut up,* and maybe nobody will notice. Other people's warmth will help you "snap out of it" and enjoy life again.

2. CONSIDER THE FEELINGS OF OTHERS. Learn to step outside yourself and see how you look to others. Mentally replay a conversation occasionally, and listen as if you were on the receiving end of your own comments. If you don't like what you hear, apologize to yourself for making you look bad to a friend. If you will only learn to consider how your *intended remark* will sound to the other fellow, you are on the high road to popularity.

3. SPREAD CHEER AND OPTIMISM. That old harbinger of doom, Gloomy Gus, is about as welcome as Hades itself. This should never be you! God *is your* partner. Act like it. Make it a habit to look at the positive side of things and spread good cheer.

4. BUT DON'T BE A "POLLYANNA." Balance is the key word here. Don't be so sweet you're sickening. It takes a little vinegar or lemon juice to make a good salad dressing, and spices liven up the dreariest foods or situations. But a little is all that's necessary. Be alive!

5. KEEP YOUR TROUBLES TO YOURSELF. To relive a negative experience in your mind as you tell someone else is to pray for another, similar experience. If that's what you want, keep right on talking. People have troubles of their own and

don't need to be burdened with yours. If you have nothing *positive and* interesting to say, try this exciting new experiment: *listen!*

6. Avoid Gossip. A janitor supply salesman specialized in maintenance companies for a time. Whenever he called on a customer he brought a juicy tale about some competitor's difficulties. He was popular at first, but after some months he began to lose customers. They realized that anybody who brings you a juicy tale about Joe, would carry Joe the same kind of story about you.

If you don't have something good to say about your friends, you too should try our new and exciting experiment. Just shut your mouth and *listen*—but don't bother to listen to *gossip,* either.

7. Be Yourself. Your most important contribution to good personal relations is to relax and be yourself. Study the Steps to an Irresistible Personality in the quiet of your den, but don't let them rob you of your spontaneity. When you are with people, just be sincere. There is plenty of time after you get home to examine your conduct and see how you might have done better. Resolve to relax and enjoy all the people you meet.

How to Tap Your Magnetic Force

Have you ever looked at a popular individual and wondered what his (or her) secret might be? He seems to draw people to himself like a magnet. Interestingly enough the secret of personal popularity really is a powerful magnetism. Some popular people use this force unconsciously, but many are in control and operate it at will.

The first positive step to increased popularity is to

recognize that, no matter who you are, *this magnetic force exists in you.* If you want a more attractive personality you must learn to intensify *your* magnetism. The Seven Steps to an Irresistible Personality were designed to stop dissipating your power. Since you have completed that part of the program you are ready to go ahead.

Part of your magnetism is generated by the physical. It operates like this simple physics laboratory demonstration:

Wind a coil of insulated wire around a core of soft iron. You have produced an electromagnet. But unless you pass an electric current through your coil it will have no force. When you start the current flowing, you find that the magnetic force grows stronger as the current is increased. However, you soon reach a limit beyond which more current doesn't help. This is the only difference between electromagnetism and personal magnetism. There is no limit to the personal variety.

How to Increase Your Personal Magnetism

Your physical body acts as the soft iron core for your personal electromagnetism, and the electricity is the vital life force. So the healthier and more vital your mind and body, the more powerful will be your attractiveness. All the work that has gone before contributes to the increased *quality of your livingness,* thus automatically intensifying your magnetic force. What we need now is a way to consciously use this magnetism to attract interesting people.

The Secret Switch

You have a tremendous secret weapon to use with your magnetism. It can serve as a trigger to turn on your most powerful attractive force. It has a very simple and pleasant name, but don't let that fool you. It is a really potent tool. It is called a *smile*.

It will pay you handsomely to get familiar with your smile. Take the trouble to understand your different ones. Stand in front of a mirror to practice. First try the kind you would give someone you don't like in response to a cursory greeting. Next try the smile you use as a reply to the comment you didn't quite hear but don't want repeated.

Now imagine that the most exciting, interesting, and attractive person you know just stepped out of your mirror and greeted you with a cheery hello. Respond with your most beautiful and meaningful smile. Notice the difference between this and the two previous ones? This one was *real*. A real smile comes from the heart and lights up your whole face. It projects good will and warmth. Practice your real smile until you are sure you can reproduce it when you want it.

Trigger Your Secret Switch Daily

Continue practicing in the mirror until you are confident that you have a winning smile. As soon as you are ready, let's see how well it works. Pick out some "sour puss" or "grouch" for a little game. I like to call it "Pin a Smile on the Sour Puss." The object is just that: to make your old grouch smile.

Contrive to meet your Sour Puss as often as possible during the next few days. Meet him (or her) in the hall, on the sidewalk, or wherever a "chance" passing is normal. Catch your "opponent's" eye with a cheerful "Good morning" or "Howdy," and flash him your most charming smile. Watch old Sour Puss' reaction. Keep score by counting the number of times you have to do it before your opponent returns your smile.

The toughest old grouch so far reported withstood attack for six consecutive times, but on the seventh he cracked—a very slight smile. From then on he responded regularly. His smile was feeble at first, but as he discovered it didn't hurt him he improved. Soon people began remarking about the grouch's improving disposition, and it became permanent. Perhaps the smile game was only a small contribution to the over-all improvement, but you can be certain *it did help*. It was a glorious victory for the student and a source of pleasure for years to come.

All this may sound a bit silly as you read it, but *it can* be a major factor in increasing your popularity. If you have any sense of humor at all, I guarantee you a real thrill when you actually pin a smile on a formidable sour puss. Try it! It's fun and good for you as well.

You can extend this little experiment and change your whole life. You have a beautiful smile that comes from your heart. *Use it!*

When you are stopped for a traffic signal, smile at the driver next to you. Smile at strangers as you pass them on the street. You might even throw in a friendly hello. Amazingly enough, you will discover that people like it. Most of them will respond with a smile and greeting of their own.

Smile as you approach the breakfast table and when you get to work. Wear it proudly everywhere you go, just like it was a brand new three carat diamond ring. It's worth more than any jewel you can imagine because of its effect on you. As you consciously wear your smile there will be a change in your disposition. You will be happier, more cheerful, and magnetic. People will be attracted by your pleasant atmosphere and want to meet you.

Be easy to meet. Greet everybody with a warm, friendly smile. Whenever you smile at a stranger, you are smiling at

God. Smile at God at every opportunity. The friendly meeting and warm greeting make up your biggest step toward popularity. *Smile!* It doesn't hurt.

Does it still embarrass you to smile at strangers? This can be overcome with a variation of Pin a Smile on the Sour Puss.

Overcoming Short Circuits

In the famous comic strip, *Li'l Abner,* the character, Evil Eye Fleegle, has a potent weapon. Called the Whammy, it is a terrible force which emanates from the evil eye of Fleegle to accomplish his nefarious ends. Fleegle's Double Whammy can knock down a bridge or explode an airplane in flight, but it is always defeated by Mammy Yokum's concentrated goodness. Mammy's power forces the Whammy back into the eye of its sender, thus rendering him temporarily unconscious or at least helpless.

When you are embarrassed by the thought of smiling at a stranger, imagine your discomfort is caused by a Whammy from the evil-eyed one. Picture the stranger as Fleegle delivering his Whammy from a big, bulging eye. Now you must be Mammy Yokum and conjure up enough concentrated goodness to defeat him.

A smile is the trigger that shoots out your concentrated goodness. Take careful aim, then—*laugh* at yourself for thinking of this bit of foolishness in the first place. The laugh pulls the trigger of your smile and your concentrated goodness is fired right into the heart of the stranger's defenses. Like Mammy Yokum, you will always beat the Whammy. With every victory you will find it that much easier to smile at the next person.

You have entered the major leagues when you can defeat the Whammy at a board of directors meeting or a meeting of the elders of your church. Life can be a lot of fun if you will let it, and if you don't take it too seriously.

Be Genuinely Interested
in Others

The second positive step toward increased popularity is: Be genuinely interested in others. In Chapter One we said the Secret of Greatness is within you, and we named it God. It is important to realize that the same Secret of Greatness, the same God, is within each of your fellow men. Therefore, any individual fellow man is exactly as important as you are. Pay attention when he talks; you might accidentally learn something.

In other words, you should spend as much effort absorbing what the other fellow has to say as you do trying to express your own ideas.

In the business world, many a fancy new system has flopped simply because the high and mighty planners failed to listen to the file clerk as she explained its basic fallacy. A brand new college graduate shrugged off the valid argument of one lowly clerk and installed his new system anyway. It was a disaster when the whole thing fell down around his ears, but the lesson has helped him on to greater accomplishments by impressing him with the value of *all* individuals.

It pays to listen with respect to everyone, but more than that, it is necessary to be considerate. The Master said, *"Inasmuch as ye have done it unto one of the least of these, my brethren, ye have done it unto me."* (Matt. 25:40)

This one is double pronged. If you are kind and considerate, even to those of lesser station, you are giving respect to God. But if you misuse just one other person, you are mistreating God. Woe unto the man who knowingly mistreats God! He is heaping trouble and misery upon himself.

Recognize the God within each of your fellow men, no matter how deeply it may be hidden. Every "stranger" you meet has something in common with you—you are both here to grow and learn to express more of God. The imbecile, the sage, the laborer, the babe, the housewife, the professor, the thief, all have something to teach you. You have only to pay the price of genuine interest. Show it in your smile and attentiveness.

Meet Each Person on
His Own Level

The third step toward increased personal magnetism is: Meet each individual on his own level as an equal. The old saying, "water seeks its own level," refers to people. In human relations equality is nearly synonymous with comfort. Don't you feel uncomfortable around people who treat you as vastly inferior? Or even superior?

The normal person will answer "yes" on both counts. But that's no reason to give the same discomfort to others. Never look or talk "down" to a man, that is to look down on the God within him. Just as important, talking "up" to someone has the effect of talking down to the God within *you*. Show each individual respect, but as an equal. The same God is in the president of the United States, the janitor, the president of General Motors, the laborer, the housewife, and the office worker.

I once closely observed an Admiral preparing to inspect during the ceremonies of a military parade. Interestingly enough, he was just as nervous about his part in the protocol and just as worried about "goofing up" as any member of the units to be inspected. In other words, he was deeply concerned about how he would look to his troops, while fully expecting them to look good to him. No doubt it was just such concern for the men in his command that made him an Admiral in the first place.

Effective organization definitely requires some form of rank, or inequality of status. Without it there is chaos because nobody has the authority or responsibility to get things accomplished. But much of the discomfort of rank can be reduced by applying a little human relations. Let the weight of your uniform or position carry the authority; *you* treat your subordinates with respect and genuine interest. You are entitled to the same respect and interest from your organizational superiors. This creates a feeling of fellowship which makes each member more comfortable and more effective.

Your personal contribution to the expression of the infinite GOD-POWER is every bit as important as anybody else's. There is no superiority or inferiority, you have only *equals*. As long as men live and work together there will be the necessity for organizational inequality. But an organization is just a group of people who have divided the authority and responsibility inherently belonging to each individual in an unequal manner, solely for the purpose of more effectively accomplishing the work at hand.

With any division of authority comes the injunction of the Master: *"But he that is greatest among you shall be your servant. And whosoever shall exalt himself shall be abased; and he that shall humble himself shall be exalted."* (Matt. 23:11-12)

As you ascend in the hierarchy of any organization, remember people will follow a Hitler out of fear or a Christ out of devotion. Resolve to do everything in your power to insure that your followers are motivated by much devotion and a minimum of fear.

Review of the Positive Steps

Let's briefly summarize the positive steps to ever increasing personal magnetism and popularity.

1. DEVELOP AND USE YOUR SMILE.
2. SHOW YOUR GENUINE INTEREST IN OTHERS AND CONSIDERATION OF THEIR FEELINGS.
3. PRACTICE EQUALITY—MAKE EACH PERSON COMFORTABLE BY MEETING HIM ON HIS OWN LEVEL.

As you consciously take these steps, bear in mind that people have an uncanny ability to sense your real feelings. How you feel in your heart about someone is every bit as important as what you say to him.

▲

Utilizing
the Magic Pyramid
for Eternal Peace of Mind

"With all thy getting, get understanding." Wealth and material abundance are wonderful, but the greatest *treasure* on earth is peace of mind. Though a man acquire millions of dollars and a vast industrial empire, there is no assurance that they will bring

chapter six
▼

him peace and happiness. Instead, he might well feel the sting described in that old Hindu saying, "The fruits of material success turn to ashes in your mouth." This is not a truism—it doesn't have to happen that way. But it probably will, unless you take the trouble to work for peace of mind, too.

At one point in my own life, I resigned a $25,000 a year presidency of a rapidly growing corporation because it seemed the only possible way to attain peace of mind. Already, the fruits of success had begun to turn to ashes in my mouth. Although I have no regrets about this action, I must admit that it was not prudent. The action was far too drastic. I was only trying to run away from myself, and naturally I couldn't. The real cure came from further spiritual study and practice, as it was necessary to clean up my personal life and change some previously habitual thought patterns. Today I know it is not necessary to quit any legitimate job in order to attain peace of mind. Mental harmony must come from within the depths of your own being, or it will not come at all.

Let's get to the root of this thing by asking: Just what do we mean by peace of mind?

Jesus called it, *"The peace that passeth all understanding."* Our language is limited in this field, but we must attempt to describe it anyway. Peace of mind is a deep sense of harmony, well-being, fulfillment, and security. It is characterized by the absence of fear, worry, or anxiety, and by the presence of a strong confidence or faith in the future. It becomes a recognizable part of the character and personality of those who learn to carry it into their everyday lives. It is a continuing experience, accurately described as a *"pearl of great price."*

This harmony cannot be achieved by the destruction of your naturally strong drives. That would be more like suicide than peace. Rather it is achieved by understanding your desires and urges and working intelligently to fulfill them.

The half-owner of a very prosperous business was leading a miserable personal life. He spent his nearly unlimited resources lavishly in the vain attempt to produce harmony, but it seemed that the more money he spent, the less he enjoyed the results. He suffered a constant agony of wondering whether his associates liked him or just his money, and he felt he had no true friends. Relief came when he realized that his apparent desire for true friendship was really a compulsion to control other people's inner thoughts. He decided to release his friends' inner beings to God, and he found a full measure of contentment in the process.

How to Achieve Balanced Growth

We must recognize that peace of mind is a function of living and is therefore dynamic in nature. You can't buy it at the corner grocery store, bring it home, put it on a shelf, forget it, and expect to own it always. It can only be produced by living in accord with the great laws of life.

Mental harmony is produced by a strong faith confidently directing the *balanced growth* in all areas of your life. Peace of mind is achieved when you learn to let that *faith* control your thoughts and actions 24 hours of every day.

A strong, well-balanced confidence must include faith in God, in yourself, in your ability to use the GOD-POWER, in your fellow man, your economic system, your government, and in your own church. The faith for which we strive is not blind or unreasoning. Rather it is a confidence built of knowledge and understanding.

Build Faith with Knowledge

Knowledge is of the *head,* but faith is of the *heart.* Faith is knowledge which has been accepted by the heart. This transference occurs when we consciously pour our love upon that which the mind has accepted as logical. In other words, open up your heart and receive the gift of the mind.

A man had been out of a job for seven weeks and his family was suffering from the severely strained finances. He had tried hard to find work, but always something seemed to be lacking. Finally he realized that the lack was his own faith.

Next morning, before starting out to go job hunting, he sat down quietly to pray. "Heavenly Father, I am a good worker. There must be a job for me somewhere. Please help me find it!"

The idea appealed to him and he sat there saying over and over, "There is a job for me." Suddenly he was interrupted by the telephone. A friend called to tell him of a local factory seeking new employees. He left the house, full of confidence, and got the job.

That which the mind knows and the heart loves, is faith. It will always work for you.

Learn to Follow the Middle Path

The faith you are building is the tool you need to achieve and maintain that *dynamic balance* which is peace of mind. Balance in this sense is nearly synonymous with moderation. About four centuries before the first Christmas, Siddhartha Gautama, called Lord Buddha, was teaching men a way of "final liberation." This beautiful philosophy is often called "The Middle Path of Buddha."

In essence Lord Buddha's message was: There is a middle path by which man may attain his highest potential. You tread this path by practicing moderation in all your actions, including moderation even in the practice of moderation.

The rewards of balance are priceless! Buddha called it Enlightenment and Final Liberation from the law of cause and effect. Jesus called it the Peace That Passeth All Understanding. They were talking about the same thing with just a slight difference in emphasis. The similarity becomes obvious when we stop to consider that:

The immediate product of balance is growth. The immediate product of balanced growth is an inner satisfaction or peace of mind, the Peace That Passeth All Understanding. And the final product of balanced growth is Enlightenment and Final Liberation from the law of cause and effect.

Gaining True Growth Through the Pyramid of Seesaws

We have said that balance is nearly synonymous with moderation. However, balance also implies a delicate judgment factor which nearly defies description. It is this discernment in your balance that lets you know when it's all right to "jump off the deep end" and "live a little." In other words, it tells you when you should be moderate in your practice of moderation.

As you use your intellect and intuition to gain the understanding necessary to build your balanced faith, you will automatically improve this judgment factor. Anytime you are in doubt, call on the God-self within for guidance. Do this by simply sitting quietly, relaxing, and knowing that your God-self is in touch with infinite wisdom at all times. Then say aloud, or just deep within your being, "The God-self within me is guiding me, now. I lovingly place my question in the hands of this God-self and accept the answer as it comes to me from the depths of infinite wisdom."

You will always get an answer. And it will be the best possible one for you and all others concerned. The God-self will never let you down.

To find one young executive on the golf course you had only to follow the trail of bent clubs in the trees. As if it were the clubs' fault he missed his shots!

Clear thinking is the essence of any mental work, and it is certainly necessary in the exercise of good judgment. It will do little good to ask for the solution to a problem not yet logically defined. You may get an answer, but will you understand it?

To our golfer's question, "What's wrong with my clubs?" the answer, "Their backswing," might not be satisfying. Fuzzy questions can only receive fuzzy answers. But clear thinking and well-digested experience are the producers of sound judgment.

The judgment factor enters particularly into the achievement of balanced growth. To understand the actual experience of growth, let's imagine a large pyramid made out of many children's teeter-totters, or seesaws. One seesaw is at the top, and each of its ends is over the midpoint of one in the row below. Therefore, there are two seesaws in the second row. But each of these ends is over the midpoint of one in the third row. So there are three seesaws in the third row, four in the fourth, etc. In each case the midpoint of a seesaw is directly below the end of one on the next row above. (*See* the illustration, page 99).

For this analogy there is an infinite number of seesaws in our pyramid. Each of us is somewhere within the maze seek-

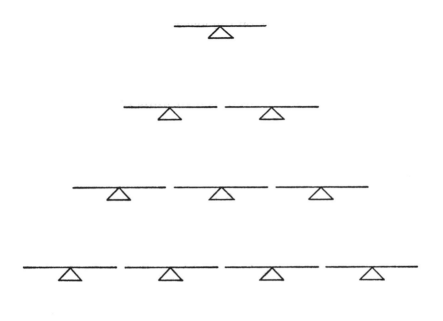

THE PYRAMID OF SEE-SAWS

ing to reach the top which symbolizes "Enlightenment" or the ultimate happiness.

Climbing the Seesaws

There is only one way to climb. You must find the balance point of the seesaw you are on. From there you can stand up and reach the end of the one in the next level up, grab it and pull yourself up onto it. Now you are one row higher, but way out of balance again. Before you can reach the next higher row, you must scramble to the balance point of your new seesaw, and if you miss, you can easily fall down a row or two.

This is a real game of skill. The higher the row of your seesaw, the more sensitive or "tricky" is its balance. You must develop a good technique on the lower rows to be able to function well on the lighter equipment of the higher.

Growth is achieved by a process quite similar to our seesaw illustration. The Life Force within impels each of us to strive upward. We flail blindly at first, while learning the basic principles of living, and our impatience causes us to make many foolish mistakes.

A young married couple discovered the "New Thought Movement" and wanted to learn more about it. They enrolled in an excellent course with a truly spiritual minister as the teacher. Wonderful new avenues of thought and expression seemed to be opening to them, but they also started to quarrel often and violently. The first stages of growth led each to lay too much stress on protecting this thing called "individuality," which is often a sophisticated term for selfishness. In the heat of the turmoil, against the advice of all their spiritual counselors, they got a divorce. Twenty-three years later they met and remarried. A little bit of balance could have saved each of them all those years of loneliness.

We grow by achieving balance at our present level of evolution and thrusting upward from its firm support. But just as with the seesaws we find we are out of balance again as soon as we reach the new level. So we must hang on tightly and work toward a new equilibrium.

This serves to emphasize the dynamic character of evolution. In order to grow it is necessary to attain balance. But growth naturally upsets the very balance from which it is spawned.

Your proper attitude toward personal growth can also be inferred from our seesaws. They normally belong to children and are used for play. In the pyramid form they have become a game of skill, but a game nevertheless. Play the game of growth to win, but remember to be a good sport—especially when you fall down.

Learn the Lesson of the Seesaws

Let's get to the meat, the basic lesson of our seesaws. Never cling to a set of circumstances or conditions and consider them the source of your peace of mind. All worldly things are bound to change; only God is changeless. What little peace you muster will be short-lived until you base it on confidence in your God-self and willingness to cooperate with Its evolutionary purpose. True peace can only come from the feeling of oneness with Deity and growth under the guidance of the Divine.

As a whole being, you are embarked on an apparently endless spiral of evolutionary experience. Everything you learn has a deeper meaning which you realize only as you acquire more knowledge.

An English friend often uses the expression, "the penny dropped." In America we would be more apt to say, "then came the dawn." Both of these common phrases illustrate our point. They mean that some small bit of information has suddenly provided the link between two previously different trains of thought. Then the penny drops—we see the interrelation, and the synthesis produces a marked increase in our understanding.

The thought that triggers the penny may be either related or paradoxical to the original knowledge. Life itself is a wondrous paradox of unity in multiplicity. But wherever you find a paradox, there is a higher truth which resolves it.

For all its multiplicity, there is only one life, just as there is only one law of gravity. Gravity expresses itself in a relatively (to us) different manner on the moon than here on Earth. Science tells us that our Astronauts landing on the moon will "weigh" only a fraction of their earth weight. Nevertheless, it is the same gravitational force manifesting itself in both places, and it also holds the moon in its orbit around the earth and the two of them in their joint orbit around the sun.

Similarly, the *one life* expresses itself as you and me, as the ant, the alligator, and the cow—and perhaps as beings far more advanced than we are, on other planets of other solar systems.

You are a whole being, but you are also a very minute part of that greater Whole Being which is the Life Force of our planet. It in turn is a minute part of the infinite being we call God, or the Life Force of the universe.

We haven't strayed as far from our study of personal peace of mind as it may appear. By contemplating the place of your own tiny evolutionary spiral in relation to those of our Earth and the mighty universe, you achieve a sense of awe and perspective which contributes much personal peace. This is another way to sense your unity with God's purpose and grow.

Your personal growth and well-being is an important part of the over-all evolution of the very Life Force of our earth. Take this deep within your being and let it intensify your urge for growth.

Don't Beat Yourself

Here is where the judgment factor in balance enters the picture again. You should always work for growth, both for yourself and any group you belong to. However, it is important not to strive too hard. Many a good football team has beaten itself because it tensed up and tried too hard. Similarly, this pyramid of seesaws we call life is a game of skill which is won only by alert, but relaxed players.

The penalty for trying to *force* growth may be easily

seen in your garden. Let's say you notice a beautiful rosebud. You get excited over its loveliness and want it to become a flower immediately, so you decide to help it. You pull it open with your fingers to unfold the gorgeous rose you know is inside. But the result is only destruction. You have no more rosebud, and no rose either. There are only the crushed and scattered petals of what might have been.

Let God Handle the Timing

A rosebud must be allowed to open in its own time, at its own speed. *You* can water and feed the plant and protect it from pests, but only the Vital Life Force can make it unfold —when God is good and ready.

And so it is with all things! The Vital Life Force is within, impelling growth. *You* nourish the desire for growth, and provide the *balance* necessary for its foundation. Then, at the right time in God's eyes, the *creative power of the universe* will provide that which you so earnestly seek.

The keys are *balance* and *faith* that the creative power of the universe is working in and through you. From the resulting growth you will experience your own "peace that passeth all understanding."

How to Grow Every Day

Let's wind up this discussion by suggesting a brief ritual that you should perform every morning for the rest of your life. When you first get out of bed, stand near an open window, preferably facing the sunrise. Take a deep breath and hold it for a few seconds. Then say aloud:

"I trust in God with all my heart, and He directs my growth in the Christ Idea—my journey along the pathway of enlightenment."

It helps to use that little thought regularly throughout the day, also. You will find the more time you give to constructive thoughts of God, the more Peace you will experience in your life. It is literally true that as you turn to God, God turns to you. As you regularly turn to God, you will find more and more light on your pathway of growth. You will learn the reality of, *"Her ways are ways of pleasantness, and all her paths are peace."* (Prov. 3:17)

"Peace I leave with you, my peace I give unto you; not as the world giveth, give I unto you. Let not your heart be troubled, neither let it be afraid." (John 14:27)

The Master Jesus' promise is a law of the universe. Accept his gift of peace. Attain it through your balanced growth, based on balanced faith. Grow, and be at peace. This is not a paradox, but the law of the universe.

"These things I have spoken unto you, that in me ye might have peace. In the world ye shall have tribulation: but be of good cheer; I have overcome the world." (John 16:33)

Your balanced growth in fulfillment in the purpose of God is your peace.

"Now, therefore hearken unto me, O ye children: for blessed are they that keep my ways. Hear instruction and be wise, and refuse it not. Blessed is the man that heareth me, watching daily at my gates, waiting at the posts of my doors. For whoso findeth me, findeth life, and shall obtain favour of the Lord." (Prov. 8:32-35)

Learn
the Secret
of Life Balance

"Thus the heavens and the earth were finished, and all the host of them. And on the seventh day God ended his work which He had made; and He rested on the seventh day from all his work which He had made."

The six chapters just concluded represent

chapter seven

the work of our first trip around the evolutionary spiral of life. Now we enter the mystic number of completion, seven. And so we dedicate Chapter Seven to rest and relaxation at the end of a creative cycle. But as always in nature, each ending is a new beginning. The end of the first trip around the spiral blends so perfectly into the beginning of the next higher level, you cannot tell where one stops and the other starts.

It is fitting, then, that we open this chapter with the allegory of Creation. *"In the beginning God created the heaven and the earth."* The work of creation took six "days," and on the seventh (mystical) day God rested. There is obviously no historical significance to this part of the allegory. Rather, its purpose is to call our attention to the importance of timing.

Know the Importance of Good Timing

There is a time for work, but also a time for rest and play. Timing is a major factor in any activity, whether you are swinging at a baseball or dodging automobiles on the freeway. Often an act itself is not nearly so important as the time at which it is performed. There is only a split-second's difference between a home run and a swinging third strike. Never under-estimate the importance of timing. It is a God-given power of discernment and discrimination that will put points on your scoreboard or money in your bank account. But *you* have to let it.

It's time now to relax. For six chapters we have worked; now let's learn to have fun. Let's relax, let go, and just plain enjoy life. Here is a truth about having fun that may surprise you: the secret is *self-discipline*, or the ability to force yourself to live up to a set of rules.

Understand the Value
of Discipline

Picture a game of football, baseball, chess, or bridge with no rules. You wouldn't have fun, you'd have chaos. Nothing ruins a bridge game quicker than a player who doesn't understand its rules and conventions.

There never was a game without rules, and no game brings pleasure until both you and your opponent have mastered its rules and theory on the field of practice. Mastery of rules and theory is only possible through discipline.

In our last chapter we considered the process of personal evolution in an illustration we might call the parable of the seesaws. One of its major points is the approach to growth as a game of skill. We have already agreed that the purpose of our whole life is evolution, so it should be apparent that we should approach life itself as a game.

In truth, the greatest challenge of all is the game of life. It, too, is not fun until you have mastered its rules and theory by practical application to daily living. Stop taking yourself so seriously. Realize that life really is a game. But it's a game of skill, not chance.

Enjoy the Game of Life

The first requirement for enjoying any game is determination to be a gracious winner and a good loser. It's particularly important to be a good loser during the trying time we might call the learning period.

In a very real sense we are learning the skills of a new game as we work with the material of this book. We are acquiring an approach to life with a degree of perspective which treats our most difficult problems as a simple game challenge. When you have gained this perspective, sportsmanship comes easily, even when you "boot" the big one. A good sport can endure poor sportsmanship from his opponent without "letting it get his goat." He understands that his own integrity and self-respect are much more important than the outcome of any one game in a long season of play.

Of course you should have a keen desire to win, but it must be *balanced* by perspective. You are acquiring all the ability and skill necessary to win the pennant in this life, so you know that no single victory is worth the price of your self-respect. Neither is the pennant. Someone may cheat you out of a game once in a while, but in reality he has only cheated himself.

The world respects a good sport as a person, but if it respects a poor sport at all, it is only as a competitor. Your temper is a substantial part of your self-respect. Take care not to lose either.

The Nature of Temper

What is this thing called temper? We all have one and, at some time in life, each of us has lost it. The word *temper* comes from the same root as *temperance* which implies *moderation* or *balance*. So to lose your temper means simply to lose your balance. But our parable of the seesaws clearly shows the result. You tumble down a few rows farther from your goal of enlightenment. The upward climb is hard enough without losing your gains to an outburst of temper.

A lost temper displays lack of self-control or discipline, and spoils the game for all those around you. It may disrupt the growth patterns of others as well as your own. If you are over twelve years old, there is no excuse for losing your temper.

But many people three or four times that age still do it. Then they will say, "I've tried and tried, but I just can't control my temper!"

First, we must understand what really takes place when you lose your temper. Something painful or frustrating happens in the objective world. Your senses (eyes, ears, etc.) carry the message to your thinking organ. You consider it for a split-second and decide you are justified in getting mad—so you "blow your top"! The key to complete control of your temper lies in this simple analysis, but you can use it only after you accept the fact that *you actually decide* to get mad. Nobody can make you mad. It is always the direct result of your own conscious decision to "blow up." This may happen so quickly you hardly realize it, but *it is your decision!*

Control of your temper is as easy as deciding not to lose it—if you have a system for relieving your tension at the critical moment.

How to Control Your Temper

This simple method will get results the first time you try it:

Promise yourself to recognize that split-second of decision making before you get mad. Let's say you've been having a bad day and have finally collapsed on the living room couch for a few minutes' respite, when suddenly your three-year-old comes running in, stumbles, and spills oatmeal all over you, couch, rug, and the cat. O.K., so you're probably justified in blowing up, but what good will it do? You *will* blow up if you don't relieve the tension, so take a deep breath and say aloud with deep feeling:

"Cock-a-doodle-doo!"

This is guaranteed to make you laugh, thus giving you a

chance to regain your perspective. It may sound silly, but it works. Certainly you will look a lot less ridiculous to those around you by shouting, "Cock-a-doodle-doo," than by cutting loose with a monstrous temper tantrum.

Once the tension is released you will regain your perspective quite easily. Remember the parable of the seesaws. After all, life is just a game, and nothing is important enough to rob you of your self-control.

After you have used this little system a few times you will be able to shout your *cock-a-doodle-doo* mentally and achieve the same results. That way nobody need know what you are doing. But it is always better to yell, "Cock-a-doodle-doo," and laugh, than to explode with a string of profanity. Now this doesn't mean we should go off balance in the other direction, either.

Nothing we have said should be construed as meaning you should become a doormat. Consider this powerful example from the life of the Master:

"Jesus went into the temple and began to cast out them that sold and bought in the temple, and overthrew the tables of the moneychangers, and the seats of them that sold doves." (Mark 11:15)

This is a classic example of timing and personal power, but it is of utmost importance to realize that Jesus *did not act in anger.* These merchants did not belong in His Father's house, so Jesus calmly but firmly evicted them.

The Secret of Personal Power

The secret of personal power lies right there. Whatever you need to accomplish, set about it *calmly, but firmly.* In the calmness your own GOD-POWER is most effective, and it will come through for you!

Our concept of meeting each person on his own level is also in point here. Some people consider it a sign of extreme weakness not to use profanity in "appropriate" places. Their friendliest greeting might be something like, "How the hell are you, you old buzzard?"

If you would reach such a person, it is necessary to at least partially speak his language. Don't be ashamed to do it, and don't consider it beneath your dignity. That would be stuffiness masquerading as dignity. It is not your words, but the feeling in your heart that is important. Suit the language and tone of voice to the occasion, but never in anger. Remember, calmly but firmly is the watchword.

The Technique of Discipline

Self-discipline is more than just control of your temper. It is the means to virtually any end. By discipline the voodoo priest gains the ability to walk on hot coals and perform many feats the uninitiated might call miracles. The same technique in the civilized world has broken the four-minute mile and will someday crack the nine-second hundred-yard dash. It produces in whatever area it is applied.

I opened this chapter by referring to self-discipline as the ability to force yourself to live up to a set of rules. For many the word *force* is the only form of discipline they understand, but there is another way which far surpasses sheer stubborn will power in achieving it. The use of will power implies that your strong desires must be curbed by the force of your will, but this is bound to create terrible internal conflicts. Psychologists tell us that strong desires repressed by the will may result in neurosis, psychosis, or simply stronger but more negative desires. If you have studied your early lessons in this work, you should be able to recite the positive approach right now. Can you?

Of course! You don't have to fight a desire with will power; you learned better than that in Chapter One. All you need do is police your motivations. Ask the desire its origin, modify it to its most positive particularization, and let it work for you instead of against you. Calmly but firmly tell any error in particularization that it no longer exists because you realize what you *really* want.

Because she loved music, a housewife resumed the piano lessons she dropped in her early teens. Very soon she began to resent the scales and finger exercises. She hated to practice them just as before. But this time she realized what she was doing to herself and decided to be an adult. She asked the urge to skip practicing where it came from, and understood it as a carry-over from the days when it was forced upon her. Then she reasoned with herself: I want to be a better musician so I can create beautiful music for myself and others. The scales and finger exercises are necessary to my development, so I want to practice them.

This dissolved the resentment so completely that she actually enjoys her scales now, and she is becoming an excellent pianist.

By constantly policing your motivations you can be the master of all your desires and never need to waste your energy in open conflict with them.

Operating Within Your Balance Area

We said that *balance is the key to peace of mind*. Since you can't enjoy yourself when your mind is troubled, it's obvious that balance is also a key to having fun. Let's elaborate on the secret of having fun all the time. We started by saying it is *self-discipline,* but that is only half the seesaw. The full secret of having fun is self-discipline *balanced by perspective.*

No activity can be fun if you give it so much importance it ties you up in knots. Conversely, no endeavor that is totally undisciplined can be enjoyable, either. In sports to try too hard is to beat yourself, but if you are too relaxed and not alert your opponent will beat you. There is a delicate area of balance between these extremes which is your source of greatest satisfaction because you know you are doing your best. Even when you lose, there is comfort in the certainty that you put forth your best effort.

Any time you are not having fun, whether at work, at play, or just resting, it is simply because you are not operating within your balance area. You are suffering from a lack of self-discipline, perspective, or both. Let's look at some mental states other than enjoyment from this standpoint.

Overcoming Boredom

When you are bored you say it is because what you are doing isn't interesting. Now whose fault is that?

Boredom is the direct result of failure or refusal to give of yourself. It is lack of desire—failure to be up for the game.

A properly self-disciplined person will find a way to give of himself in any situation, and that very giving will eradicate his boredom. Consider the plight of the tree. Nobody has to entertain it, and it can't even go for a walk. It must be content just to *be* and to *grow.* A tree's happiness must come only from its growth and from just being a tree. So does yours!

If it takes more to make you happy than simply to be and to grow, you are missing the boat. Jesus had an interesting way of putting it: *"Verily, I say unto you, Whosoever shall not receive the Kingdom of God as a little child, he shall not enter therein."* (Mark 10:15)

This doesn't mean you should be childish. But you should be filled with the wonder, awe, and curiosity of a little child. Then you will be too busy growing to be bored.

What to Do About Self-Pity

Feeling sorry for yourself is simply a lack of perspective. In the game of life we often suffer setbacks. Of course you can't win them all, but if you did life would get pretty dull. Remember it's necessary to make the law of averages work for you. Victory can go only to the man who gets up one more time than he is knocked down.

A young married couple sought help saying, "We're in a rut and the only way out seems to be a divorce."

To the question, "Whose fault is it?" they finally answered, their own. Each had chosen to make married life a rut by looking only at the sameness. They were looking at a rosebush and seeing only the thorns.

They decided to start looking for—and loving—the roses. They chose to use the Formula for Personal Creation to magnify the good in their marriage. They have both grown into greater understanding of marriage and life itself by this simple process.

Getting Rid of Anger

Anger is just your negative response to sudden loss of perspective caused by a lack of discipline. Mere control of your temper is not enough. If you are seething with barely controlled rage you're probably doing more damage to your body than if you actually let it blow.

We must strive for the mental agility that enables us to

see the humor in situations that previously made us mad. If you don't see the humor, add your own with a *cock-a-doodle-doo* and laugh away the negative reaction. Always return to balance quickly, playing life as a game. Every incident that tends to make you mad is a wonderful opportunity for growth. Don't lose your balance. *Grow* instead!

How to Handle Embarrassment

Your timing was off, so you "goofed." So what? If you do something silly, just step outside yourself and see it as it appears to others. Laugh with them and enjoy it. Nothing is better for your perspective than a good laugh at yourself. It helps relieve your tension and endears you to your fellow man.

Embarrassment is lack of perspective, whether it stems from a goof or feelings of inadequacy. The Admiral and his entourage came briskly down the corridor. With proper deference, a young Ensign snapped to attention. But he was too close to the wall and fell flat on his face. As he scrambled to his feet he knew he must make a quick choice. He could stand there red in the face and hope everybody would disappear, or—he chose to laugh with them. He smiled and said, "You sure made an impression on me, sir."

The Admiral returned the smile, stopped his party and shook hands. A touch of humor will always bring pleasure out of an otherwise embarrassing situation.

You Can End Loneliness

Loneliness is akin to boredom. It stems from the same lack of willingness to give of the self. This is lack of self-discipline. Always look for a way to give when you are lonely or bored. These states can't exist when you are giving.

Many worthy charities are in need of volunteer workers,

and your church can always use another person to call on new additions to the neighborhood or those in need of help and encouragement. Or, some lonely day, just stroll down to your neighborhood Laundromat. Talk to the little children who must entertain themselves while mother is busy with the wash. Help someone get her laundry folded and into the car. Use your smile along with the other principles of popularity we have studied. You may start a deep and lasting friendship. Certainly you will be surprised at how little giving it takes to end loneliness.

Never Give In to Despair

It takes discipline to maintain the balanced faith that keeps you from giving up. Despair is self-pity that has fallen down a few extra rows of seesaws. But the beauty of being so low is the first few steps back up are so easy. You can *bounce* back!

The young athlete was in his first track meet, running the middle distance. It seemed that he was a hundred yards behind at the half-way mark and the feeling of despair was tremendous. But he set his jaw and ran harder. He started to gain on the leader and found new strength. Opponents literally faded in the stretch and he actually won. What if he had given in to his despair?

You will never know how spent your opponent may be unless you keep trying. Don't give up, *bounce up!* Turn certain defeat into victory because you're too dumb to give up. It's fun, and life will seem much better for that little extra effort.

The Meaning of Restlessness

It's a peaceful evening and you are stretched out on the

couch with a good book. You should be contented and happy, but instead you're miserable. Something keeps asking you, "What is life all about?" or, "Do I really have a reason for living?" or, "Why should I care about anything?"

This is the yearning of the Spirit within you for growth. It can only be cured by a well-balanced pattern of spiritual seeking. Alcohol, parties, and sex may temporarily relieve this restlessness, but it will return ever stronger until your spiritual longing is satisfied. A book may point the way, but only your efforts can bring the needed growth.

Often when you have done everything you can to insure the success of a project and now it must be left to the decisions of others, you get the jitters. Doubts come from every side, and if you accept them, they will destroy your peace of mind or even the project itself.

Self-discipline will see you through this one, too. Train yourself to refuse restless, doubting thoughts. We spent a whole chapter on eliminating fear and its relatives. *Use it!* When your project has reached the point of release into the laps of the gods, it's no time to spoil your efforts with worry and doubt.

A parakeet fancier produced a short course on the raising of these colorful birds. He soon received a letter from a reputable publisher asking if he would like to make a book out of it. The prospect of furthering the cause of his feathered friends made him wildly enthusiastic, so he quickly replied in the affirmative.

Doubts Can Be Overcome

Then came the first doubt. What if they aren't interested after all? Following the principles of Chapter Two, he told himself that this was God's project and of course the publisher would stay interested. Then he demonstrated his faith by assembling what he guessed would be the preliminary material the publisher would request in his positive reply. The doubt was thus defeated, and in a reasonable time the request came. Because of his preparation, he was able to respond by return mail.

Now the forces of doubt moved up their heaviest artillery and fired at him with everything they had. The work is no good—the publisher won't understand what you are trying to do—who says you can write a book anyway—you don't have any pull with the publisher, how do you expect to get your work accepted?—maybe it's all some kind of a racket—literally hundreds of doubts came all at the same time.

Again he began his defense with the statement, "This is God's project."

Next he refuted each doubt in turn—God's work *is* good —certainly the publisher will understand God—of course God can write a book through me—God has all the pull we need with the publisher—God is not a racket—each doubt was "clobbered" as soon as it popped up. Now he needed another act of faith, so he started to write his book.

He was starting the second chapter when the letter came acknowledging receipt of his preliminary material and saying it must be reviewed by the editorial staff. This would take from four to six weeks and there was no indication that the result would be favorable. But by now he had the problem licked. He could already see the finished book in his mind's eye as he spent all his free time writing.

With this attitude the GOD-POWER had an effective channel through which to operate. The happy ending came as he was starting the eighth chapter. It was a friendly letter enclosing a contract for the publication of his book—with no strings attached.

You will always have a happy ending if you discipline yourself to keep working at your problem with energy and faith until it is solved. Never accept doubt. Replace it with balanced faith!

The Secret of Full
Life-Enjoyment

In summary, the secret of really enjoying life is *self-discipline balanced by perspective.* Discipline is the tool you use to control your emotions, while perspective builds that delicate judgment factor which tells you when to relax your discipline and truly enter into the spirit of the game. When you have balanced these two, you are in a position to intelligently exercise your freedom of choice. Choose to be happy and have fun. You will find it done unto you as you have chosen.

> Happy is the man that findeth wisdom, and the man that getteth understanding. For the merchandise of it is better than the merchandise of silver, and the gain thereof than fine gold. She is more precious than rubies: and all things thou canst desire are not to be compared unto her. Length of days is in her right hand; and in her left hand riches and honor. Her ways are ways of pleasantness, and all her paths are peace. She is a tree of life to them that lay hold upon her: and happy is every one that retaineth her. (*Prov. 3:13-18*)

She is also the point of balance between self-discipline and perspective. Play your game of life for the sheer joy of growth, and suddenly you will realize that you *are* having fun all the time.

▲

Let the Growth Machine Make You Important

"Ye call me Master and Lord: and ye say well; for so I am. If I then, your Lord and Master have washed your feet; ye also ought to wash one another's feet. For I have given you an example that ye should do as I have done to you."

There are many

chapter eight

▼

levels of meaning in the symbolic act of washing the disciples' feet. However, for this study we need consider it simply a personal elaboration on His teaching given to the multitudes:

"And whosoever shall exalt himself shall be abased; and he that humble himself shall be exalted. . . . But he that is greatest among you shall be your servant."

Some people are confused by this beautiful teaching of the Master. They read it and conclude that their reason for living is to serve others. But this thinking hits a blank wall when you ask the logical question: If you are here to serve others, then why are the others here?

Don't get entangled in such circular thinking, or we may have to invent a new beatitude, something like: Blessed are they who think in circles, for they shall be known as intellectual wheels.

How to Put Service to Work for You

Service to others is an important part of your life, but it is necessary to understand its true purpose as a function of the reason for existence. This can be drawn from our early study of the Formula for Personal Creation. Let's restate the first step:

1. *Understand God's purpose and unify with it.*

We agreed that God's purpose for us is growth or evolution, individually and collectively. This is the wedge that lets us break into the circular thinking on service. Your *purpose* is to *grow*. The *method* of achieving growth is service to others. Of course others are here to grow, and their *method,* too, is service. But this makes sense. The product of mutual service is mutual growth.

Service is important as a means to an end, not an end in

itself. We should recognize our need to serve as a desire, and subject it to the usual tests. In short, we must police the motivations behind our urge to serve.

By calling growth the product of service we must consider the normal earthly rewards as the by-products. Be careful of your attitude towards the resulting money, recognition, glory, and status. Place your emphasis on the true goal, not on the by-products, but maintain your balance.

The motivation is often more important than the act itself. This can readily be seen in the case of money. Strangely enough, most people will pay very little attention to you unless you expect a substantial payment for your services.

A junior executive lost his job as a result of a corporate merger. He easily arranged for interviews with good firms who needed talent, but he was turned down regularly. When he sought professional guidance he learned that his willingness to take a very low starting salary was holding him back. Prospective employers were looking for exceptional men and they were afraid of him because of his low price tag. He raised his financial sights and began to positively *sell* his *abilities*. Almost immediately, he landed a better job than the ones which had previously been refused him.

Similarly, you may accept recognition, status, and glory as the means to achieve opportunities for greater service. But if you accept them as ends in themselves, you are heading for a downfall. Growth produces importance, but importance tends to destroy further growth.

How to Operate Your
Growth Machine

We might look at *service* as a machine which produces growth. The raw materials are other people's needs, and the

power which drives the machinery is your own GOD-POWER or
Vital Life Force. You have a bright and shiny machine all
hooked up and apparently ready to operate. Certainly there is
an ample supply of raw material, but there is still a missing
ingredient. You wouldn't try to operate a physical machine until you were sure it was properly lubricated. Our allegorical
machine deserves the same good treatment, and the lubricant
is *humility*.

We must "oil" our growth machine thoroughly, but take
care not to over-do and thus gum up the working parts.

Let's turn on our growth machine and watch it work.
Listen to its smooth, well-lubricated operation. It is producing
growth efficiently and effectively, but look out! The by-product
is this thing called *importance* and it acts as a powerful solvent.
If we are not careful it will wash away all our lubricant. It will
so dilute our humility that there remains no protection for the
moving parts, and the resulting friction will grind us to a
screeching stop.

We can avoid this disaster by carefully collecting the
by-product in bottles or cans where it cannot dilute our humility. This process of bottling does more than just prevent disaster. There is always a good market for importance balanced
by undiluted humility. Shortly we will be able to sell it for
enough to buy bigger and better opportunities for service, and
this will start the growth cycle all over again but at a higher
level on the great upward spiral of life.

The truly important man has a humility which is born
of union with the purpose and consequently, the power of God.
It is that humility which confidently states:

> Believest thou not that I am in the Father, and the
> Father in me? The words that I speak unto you I speak not
> of myself: but the Father that dwelleth in me, he doeth the

> works. Believe me that I am in the Father, and the Father
> in me: or else believe me for the very work's sake. (*John
> 14:10-11*)

Humility is never weakness or timidity; it is power and strength, intelligently controlled. It was still speaking in Jesus as he continued His discourse:

> Verily, verily, I say unto you, He that believeth on
> me, the works that I do shall he do also; and greater works
> than these shall he do; because I go unto my Father. And
> whatsoever ye shall ask in my name, that will I do, that the
> Father may be glorified in the Son. (*John 14:12-13*)

We stressed balance as a prerequisite to growth. Humility is an excellent example. It is a balance between arrogance and timidity, between conceit and inferiority, and between ambition and defeatism. Only with humility do we insure that our growth machine is well lubricated and thus able to serve effectively. And by effective service we obtain the by-product, importance, which is the price of opportunities for greater service.

From service comes growth, and thus the fulfillment of your purpose in life. It should be obvious, then, that an opportunity to serve is a precious commodity and should never be taken lightly. Great opportunities come only after you have demonstrated your ability and willingness to handle the lesser ones.

A young man was being considered for a very good job as supervisor of a large group of janitors. Part of the examination of his qualifications was a requirement to demonstrate the technique of cleaning a toilet. He refused to put his hands into it because he felt that would be beneath his dignity. And as a result the job was given to a man of lesser knowledge but greater willingness.

The young man's action was ridiculous. God is as much the substance of the dirt in a toilet as that of a rose or the fresh mountain air. If you feel otherwise you will have difficulty in accepting precious opportunities for service of a so-called "degrading" nature. Somebody has to change the world's dirty diapers, and you can be sure the man who does it is greater than the one who refuses because it is "beneath his dignity." God is never beneath anybody's dignity—don't ever forget it. The grime of honest toil will wash off your hands and body, but the soil in your heart from refusing your share of life's "messy" work will remain until it is washed away by the sweat of loving service.

The world pretty much judges the value of your service by the price you are able to command for it. There are some "spiritual" people who will argue that this is a "lousy" system, but they are simply spewing out their sour grapes.

The attendance of a little church dwindled steadily for over a year, causing near panic to the minister because he looked upon the congregation as his source of livelihood. In his sermons he regularly criticized the absent members and complained that they were too interested in sex, drinking, and money grubbing to care about spiritual things. Even worse, he complained regularly from the pulpit about the scantiness of the collection. His attitude became so negative it was a living implication that God is mean and stingy. By this time his services were being attended by less than a dozen staunch regulars.

He finally sought help from other spiritual leaders, and was met with the injunction: Look to the needs of your congregation, not the needs of the church. Any church that even partially satisfies a real need will prosper. Give the people what they need, not what the minister wants them to have, and your church cannot but grow and flourish.

He was deeply hurt at first, but he took these thoughts into the silence and prayed for guidance. With much prayer and meditation over several months, he transformed his personality to one of faith and radiance. With this change came the rebuilding of his group as a beacon for all mankind.

How the Law of Attraction and Repulsion Acts

We said the way to increase your income is to be of better service, but now we must shift our emphasis to the reasons behind your service. If you have all the money you can possibly need or use in a lifetime, it's still necessary. Vast wealth is a curse if you let it reduce your willingness and desire to be useful. You will never be happy or important if you are not in tune with God's great evolutionary purpose, and you cannot grow without serving.

Let's be sure we understand what *service* really means. To serve is to give of yourself—your interest, time, and physical effort; your creative ideas, loyalty, and moral support.

Giving of yourself in service produces growth by the action of a basic law of the universe. We learned that our whole being is a magnet, attracting or repelling experiences and things according to the way we polarize our thought patterns. We may state the law in its simplest form as: That which you give, you attract; and that which you withhold, you repel.

Many people never learn this simple law. They go through life complaining that they always lose the things which are dearest to them. They hate to go to work, so they never advance. They hate to pay their bills, so they never seem to have enough money. They cling to their children with "smother" love, so the kids grow up hating them. Some even hoard food until it rots.

There is an old saying, "You can't eat your cake and have it, too." But the truth is, the only way to have it is to eat it or give it away. To cling to it is to let it spoil and be completely wasted. And so it is with all parts of life.

This law is so important it bears emphasis. We will call it the Law of Attraction and Repulsion, and state it this time in its more accurate form:

That which you give, or would willingly give, you attract; and that which you withhold, or strongly desire to withhold, you repel.

Let's examine humility in the light of this great law. To be humble is to give importance to others, but your very act of giving it increases your own. To be arrogant or conceited withholds importance from others and so diminishes your own.

Never Try to Steal Growth

The same law brings us an important warning. Never try to grow at someone else's expense. Reaching the top over the broken bones of your fellow men brings certain disaster. Nothing will make you fall faster than stealing growth from someone else. It is the certain action of *universal law* that in the final analysis you can only steal from yourself.

A man built a big business with payoffs and by cheating his employees, customers, and the government. For eleven years he enjoyed only the best of everything, and he thought he was getting away with it. Then came the heart attack. He lost everything, and came out of the hospital in debt. But the long weeks on his back helped him to gain a new understanding of himself. He resolved to start again, but this time in harmony with the laws of life. He found a backer and built a new business on a legitimate basis. Today he is happy, *healthy,* and more prosperous than before.

The natural laws of the universe cannot be violated without the inevitable price, right down to the last atom's worth. The game of life isn't won or lost in a month, a year, or even in just one lifetime. But it is finally won by growth.

The Secret of Personal Importance

In summary, real importance is a natural by-product of growth, but if you let it go to your head, it will destroy the very growth that is its source. Knowing that service is the means of achieving growth, we are ready to state the secret or principle of personal importance:

The secret of achieving personal importance is service, balanced by humility.

To seek importance for its own sake is fruitless vanity, but to accept its responsibilities as a means to more effective service and growth is to fulfill your purpose on earth. A great man seldom realizes his own importance, and certainly never has time to worry about it. An old Chinese proverb explains it well: "Never run after a horse. If it's yours it will come back to you." Seek importance and she flees from you like a frightened animal, but forget her in loving service and she returns to eat out of your hand.

▲

How to Turn
Every Acquaintance
into a True Friend

Let's start looking
for the deeper meanings
of friendship by deciding
what it isn't. There are
many relationships based
upon economic or social
necessity, but it is rare
to find a spark of true
friendship in them. When
the needs of the parties
are not almost perfectly

chapter nine

▼

balanced economically, emotionally, intellectually, and even physically, there generally develops some sort of a dependency relationship. Some examples of the normal manifestations are: teacher-pupil, purchasing agent-salesman, husband-wife-child, owner-employee, or politician-voter.

If true friendships do develop out of one of these, it is in spite of, rather than because of them. The old "a friend in need is a friend indeed" bromide is dangerous because it tends to cause budding friendships to degenerate into some form of dependency. I don't mean to condemn dependency relationships. They are necessary and good, in and for themselves, but they should not be confused with true friendship.

Look for Growth

The essence and strength of true friendship is the coming together of two reasonably whole beings not out of necessity, but *affinity*. Like everything else on the earth plane, perfection in this area is unattainable; but the closer we approach it, the nearer we are to the ideal friendship. This special form of true love grows out of the act of sharing experience and emotion for the sheer joy of the sharing, with no strings attached. Real growth is to be found in this relationship, and it is mutual just as the enjoyment of the sharing itself.

Like our "growth machine" this is another example of a product and a by-product which tends to inhibit further production. Joyous mutual sharing of emotional experience produces wonderful friendship, and its by-product is real growth for both parties. But the very dynamics of the growth will cause the friends to grow together or apart; there will be no standing still. The mutual affinity will often wax and wane, improving or straining the relationship.

Many times we see what seems to be the tragic result.

One friend's affinity decreases while the other's increases. This is most evident in the "broken heart" left to one party of a terminated romance, while the other blithely moves on to greener pastures.

This sort of occurrence is not at all tragic. Indeed, it is natural and good. Friendship is a dynamic thing which must wax and wane as its participants travel the pathway of evolution. Though romance is a special kind of friendship, it must be looked upon with the same adult eye that views any other personal relationship. Enjoy it while it lasts. It may even develop into an ideal marriage. But if it breaks up instead, have no regrets. Sometimes the greatest act of love is to release the other to God.

It is as absurd to cling to old, dying friendships as to refuse to make new ones. Nothing in the universe is static. Our whole solar system is moving through space at tremendous speed, in its own way making new friendships and letting others cool off. Some friendships endure for a lifetime, growing in depth as the years go by. They are the story book kind and are beautiful beyond description. But there are others that, in their own time and place, are equally wonderful though they last only a few hours.

True friendship can survive only as long as it approaches the ideal of mutuality. It is enriched as both parties strive quietly for that independence of feeling which brings one nearly whole being to meet another and simply commune.

By the very nature of the relationship it is impossible to have a large number of close friends at any one point in time. In fact, the more close friends you think you have, the more probable it is that you don't have any.

One of the essential elements in the building and maintenance of deep friendship is time spent together. Proximity normally encourages the development of mutual understanding and rapport. This is why so many secretaries wind up marrying the boss. It is also the reason divorce is so painful after many years of marriage.

After twenty years of married life the vast difference in their growth caused one couple to decide they could no longer stand living together. After the divorce proceedings were completed, each commented that there had been a feeling of hurt inside as much for the other's loneliness and confusion as for his own. This shows the strength of rapport which is built by years of close association, even under trying conditions.

How to Warm Your Acquaintanceships

The first step from acquaintanceship to friendship is the development of some degree of mutual understanding—the feeling that each pretty well knows what makes the other "tick." Many relationships slow down at this point as the participants find their personal approaches to life not totally compatible. The great depths of mutual feeling probably cannot be achieved, but the degree of understanding is more than normally felt for a mere chance acquaintance. Give thanks to God for this extra taste of life and term it a warm acquaintance.

Many people go through life forming warm acquaintances, calling them friendships, and never bothering to look for anything more from this aspect of life. They tend to live only on the surface, calling all members of their own sex "buddy," and the opposite sex "honey." They probably tried to go deeper into friendship one time and were terribly hurt for their trouble. That hurt came because they had established a dependency relationship and tried to call it friendship.

Though George was 20 years her senior, he married Patsy after a two week courtship. He loved her deeply, but soon became uneasy about the difference in their ages. He grew steadily more possessive as the months passed. Finally he couldn't stand to let her out of his sight even long enough to go to the grocery store. Naturally, this caused many fights. To keep from being smothered, she finally left him after six years of marriage. Night after night he cried on her doorstep and pleaded with her to come back to him. She was wise to refuse.

If George had decided to be a whole being instead of an emotional dependent, there would have been no hurt when the time came to release her to her highest good. Of course, if he had avoided being possessive he would never have lost her.

After studying these principles George realized it was worth the effort to try again. He attracted a wonderful woman nearer his own age, and they are enjoying a very happy life together.

How to Build an Elementary Friendship

Warm acquaintanceship turns into elementary friendship with the development of mutual trust. In this process it is important to remember the Law of Attraction and Repulsion. Try giving trust, not just verbally, but by the way you act. What you give a person, he tends to return in kind. More often than not, the simple act of giving of yourself is all that is necessary to launch the deeper relationship.

If you are occasionally rebuffed or even cheated, so what? You tried! There will be many rich experiences along the way to make up for it—if you don't give up. As you keep trying, you will develop another group, much smaller in number than your warm acquaintances, that you can accurately categorize as friends. This is a worthwhile end in itself, but it can also be the beginning of a much richer experience.

Out of your group of friends there will emerge one or two with whom this mutual understanding and trust grows into a personal, living *love*. We can understand this personalized love as a magnification of your general love for all of God's creations. Think of God's general love as being focused by the lens of your consciousness, just as the general givingness of the sun's rays may be focused by a magnifying glass. You regularly experience and give God's impersonal love to all creatures. When you use your individualized consciousness as a lens to focus this love-energy upon one particular person, a whole new field of experience opens to you.

How to Share Infinite Love

Each of us is like a combination of a lens and a reflector. In this illustration the sunshine of God's love is shining on the whole world as always. With the lens of personal interest and concentration, you can focus this general love into a point of burning fire. As you direct this love-energy to your object, he (or she) will feel the heat of it. Then depending upon the blending or clashing of your inner personalities, he (or she) will either try to escape the discomfort, or start to respond.

Your love object responds by using the mirror part of his being to reflect back to you a great deal of the love-energy sent to him. This naturally improves your focus and thereby increases the total amount of love entering the system. Then as your object receives the greater dose of love-energy, he begins to focus his own lens on you, thus bringing in even more. As the rapport increases you each focus more and more love upon the other, and in turn reflect more back to the other. There is no limit to the total amount of love that can be built up by such a process.

When such a build-up of love-energy is shared by two

sincere individuals, the product is a depth of personal relationship which must be experienced to even be imagined. An intangible something is added to the whole universe when you share this depth of feeling. It is truly an approach to God.

Some people may tell you it's dangerous or wrong to build a relationship of this depth with anyone. They say, if you let somebody get that close to you, he may hurt you deeply, or his death might be more than you can bear.

We will prove that there can be no hurt from *real* love. But for now let's just say it's worth the risk simply to be a part of something so worthwhile. We are only on the threshold of understanding the depth and value of this intimate friendship. Let's review the process and let our new perspective carry us into a unique experience.

How to Insure the Formation
of a Friendship

Your personal magnetism brings a new acquaintance into your life. You sense a mutual affinity, so you spend time together learning what makes each other tick. A degree of mutual understanding is generated and you reach the stage of warm acquaintance. In time you find your individual approaches to life quite compatible. The affinity is still there, so you give and receive a sincere trust. We have called this stage an elementary friendship. It is here you may feel an increasing affinity and begin to bathe the other in a stream of pure personalized love. This love is really from God, but your personalization increases its intensity tremendously. As your friend responds, the intensity of the love between you grows and grows. It knows no bounds!

(Please don't be confused by the connotations of lust or sex that some people hang on this word *love*. What we mean to

convey is a platonic concept of pure givingness. Any self-grati-
fication involved is limited to the vicarious enjoyment of the
fulfillment or growth of the other person.)

As this mutual love unfolds into the depths of true
friendship, you approach very near to God because you learn to
get outside yourself and literally live in and through the other
person. God lives in and through each of us and is each one
of us. By achieving the depth of feeling necessary to "become"
your friend, you are living as God. This is the gateway to the
unique experience we promised.

As you learn by loving to live in and through another
person, you are becoming a practical mystic. You now hold the
true mystic experience in your hand.

Try this experiment: Sit with your friend, focusing and
reflecting the love-energy. Seek the complete rapport. For the
time, become your friend; think his thoughts as him, rather
than as yourself. Experience his desires as your own, harbor his
hopes and dreams. *LIVE completely outside yourself, as your
friend!*

How to Transfer the
Rapport to God

The beauty of rapport is its ability to be extended. Once
you have established a true oneness with another individual
you have made a basic change in your whole psychological
make-up. You have demonstrated to your ego the great service
it can perform by simply "melting." You now know that by
relinquishing your hard shell of individuality you do not die.
Rather you live much more intensely, but as an integral part
of a new "group-being" which is created by the deep rapport.

When your ego accepts this lesson, you will find it easy
to transfer or extend the original oneness to other persons and

things. Practice coming into rapport with your friend and then expanding the at-one-ment to include all of God's creation. One day when you realize your attunement with the whole of creation, it will burst into a living, vibrant *oneness with God*. This experience is not of the intellect. It is felt at the center of your being and radiates in splendor into every corner of your existence.

Why We Must Live Outwardly

This oneness with God is *the kingdom of heaven*. You find it within yourself of course, but one path to its realization has proved to be outgoingness.

There are mystics who claim to go directly within and reach God at the center of their own beings. This is the path of introversion. It will undoubtedly work, but it is more the path for the Oriental mind. The minds and personalities of the members of our more outgoing, material, Western civilization are oriented to action, rather than contemplation of the navel. It is only logical that we should have an easier time finding God by giving our love outwardly than by shutting out the world and trying to live only within.

I personally have the deepest respect for the true mystic experience, no matter how it is produced. But there are two good reasons why I recommend the way of outside rapport.

First is the idea of giving, rather than taking. If you become a confirmed introvert while seeking God deep within yourself, you are taking yourself away from the world, refusing to share your livingness. But what you withhold, you tend to lose. So how can you achieve a full-fledged mystic experience by intensifying your livingness while driving it away? It must be harder than the way of givingness.

The second reason for the path of outside rapport is

even more obvious. People have been known to spend a whole lifetime seeking the mystic experience without success. It seems to me you would feel pretty stupid lying there dead in some old hermitage or cave—having spent a lifetime cooped up inside yourself looking for something you never did find. Could anything be more futile? But if you spent the same lifetime seeking the same experience by giving of yourself in friendship, many lives would be enriched along the way. Thus the fact of your failure to achieve the ultimate would seem relatively insignificant.

In finding oneness with God through the medium of deep personal friendship, we have a beautiful and practical example of the relationship between the universal and the particular. Many centuries ago Hermes taught, "As above, so below." Individual man is a reflection of the whole universe.

Though the pathway to God is outward givingness, the key to understanding lies within your own heart. We have called it the GOD-POWER within you. As God lives by giving existence to the universe, so the individual finds his true livingness by attaining rapport with all God's creation. Thus we find the essence of true friendship is *friendship with God.*

The Five Steps to True Friendship

We will summarize by briefly stating the five steps to true friendship:

Step 1. Pick out one or two of your warmest acquaintances, for whom you seem to have the most affinity. Give freely of your trust to these people. Keep demonstrating your trust until you are sure it is mutual.

Step 2. Give of *yourself* to this relationship. Focus the wonderful love-energy of God upon your friend and feel it intensify as it is reflected back and forth between you. Work for rapport. Think your friend's thoughts; share his aspirations, hopes, and dreams.

Step 3. Go out through your own heart and enter into his. Literally become your friend for a time. This is the ultimate in individual rapport.

Step 4. Expand this individual rapport until you feel your oneness with all of God's creation. Love it, and feel the whole universe living in your heart. Suddenly you will realize a personal oneness with God. You reach the universal through the keyhole of the particular.

Step 5. *Use it!* Don't hide your light under a bushel. Come back down the mountain into life, knowing all men as your brothers. Oriental religions may value the mystic experience as a means to achieve freedom *from* the world, but we should see it as the way to achieve freedom *in* the world.

Share your new light with the world. The more you give, the more you will have. Give of yourself in loving service to mankind. There is no ultimate in growth. So you may achieve the mystic experience! Even then it's not time to lie down and die, or even rest. *Serve!*

To be a true mystic is a wonderful experience, but we must never forget *we are here in this world.* Take care how you appear to others. If you picture the great goal of your religion as some state that appears to be goggle-eyed, gibbering idiocy, you may discourage or disillusion a host of practical people who are still on the path. We teach more by the example of our lives than by the words of our mouths. Live to be your best example of everything you believe and share the depths of mystic feeling only with those who are ready.

Live and work in the practical world, but enjoy God's friendship as an integral part of life. Your comfort and strength is: If God is my friend, who can be my enemy? Once you have felt the intimate companionship of God, you will never release it. It is truly a "pearl of great price."

> A new commandment I give unto you, that ye love one another; as I have loved you, that ye also love one another. By this shall all men know that ye are my disciples, if ye have love one to another. (*John 13:34-35*)

Love is the essence of life itself. Live!

How to
Find Your
True Place in Life

We shall once more study the part of life which you devote to making a living. This time our interest is in the satisfaction and fulfillment you should derive from your efforts. Psychologists tell us that job satisfaction is a necessary element of mental health.

chapter ten

Regardless of the size of your monthly paycheck, you *need* to derive real pleasure from the actual performance of the many tasks which make up your job. On this earth plane there may be some irksome duties connected with it, but you are *entitled* to enjoy *most* of every working day.

Your Attitude Controls Boredom

A man quit seven good jobs in less than one year because he was bored. He had a vague feeling that he was not in his true place, and thought he would live happily ever after if he could just land the right job. He somehow expected the heavens to open up and a white dove come to him with a special assignment from on high. And more, he expected all the necessary skills and training to come with it simultaneously. *Utter nonsense!*

He began to get ahead when he finally realized that each person on earth is in the position he has attracted to himself. In a very real sense, he was in his true place every moment of every day. His position was exactly what he had earned and attracted to himself by all his own past work, play, thoughts, aspirations, feelings, and actions. This knowledge *gave him the power* to create a better life for himself. He will continue to progress as long as he *uses* his new knowledge.

Your Power to Build a Better Life

Just as that man, *you have the power to build a better life*. Take time to review your past from birth to the present. As you measure your thoughts and actions by the principles we have been studying, you will realize what has led you to your present station. Be honest with yourself. Don't blame someone else because you are not embarked upon a glorious career. So your mother was sick and you had to drop out of medical school; or maybe Sally did get pregnant and you had to marry her instead of going on to that "rah rah" college of your dreams; or there was a depression when you graduated from high school, and you spent your college years in a C.C.C. camp. You acted according to the best sense of values you had at the time. And no part of that is holding you back now! Don't use the past as a crutch or a convenient excuse for failure. Make it your stepping stone to glorious success. It's all in your point of view.

Some people will even complain: "But I was born poor!" So was Abraham Lincoln and a host of other greats of our history! Even the circumstances of your birth were the result of your past thoughts, feelings, and actions, but we will go into that later. For now we are content to recognize that wherever you find yourself in this life, *it's your own fault you're there.*

Look at the wonder of that truth! It doesn't condemn you, it sets you free. If your present situation is the result of your own thoughts, feelings, and actions, then *you alone* have the power to control your future. You acquire the authority to control your life simply by accepting the responsibility for the results you are creating.

How shall you exert this control over your future? By taking control of yourself in the present! You are no longer entitled to say, "I can't help feeling _____" Oh, yes *you can!* Perhaps a baby can't help all sorts of things, but an adult can and does *choose* his thoughts, feelings, and actions.

Which are you? If your answer still has to be fuzzy, you see clearly why you feel you haven't found your true place.

Life is like an automobile. A child at the wheel may proceed aimlessly with much danger of mishap. Or he may not be able to get the thing started and so must sit and wait to be rescued.

Don't be a child at the wheel of your life. Grow up and drive like an adult! Develop self-discipline in any weak areas of your make-up. Put real purpose and direction into your existence.

Once you are comfortably in control of your vehicle, you can steer it in any direction that appeals to you. But you must start where you are now! You can't skip any part of the trip. Though you may move at great speed, you must actually travel over every inch of your chosen road.

You can't wish for a better life and expect it to happen with no effort on your part. You must always give something in exchange for personal progress. But the gift usually turns out to be something you didn't need in the first place.

The Lesson That Frees You

If some area of your life seems dull or unpleasant, study it carefully. Seek its price—what must you pay for progress? There is always a lesson, and you are stuck with the problem until you have learned it.

So often the student cries out in anguish: "When will I be free from this drudgery?"

And the Master replies: "When you have learned the lesson, my son."

In the process of divorcing her fifth husband a woman cried out, "Why must I go through this agony so many times?" As she reviewed her familiar misery, she suddenly realized that her attitude toward marriage had always been, "What's in it for me?" She began working to change her approach to one of givingness and promised herself to avoid situations of the old kind. She soon met a wonderful man and entered into her sixth marriage with a sincere desire to give. They have been ecstatically happy for many years, solving each problem by giving to each other.

Never run away from a problem until you are sure you have learned its lesson. A little reflection on the course of your life will reveal the bitter-sweet truth that:

You must face the same problem, over and over again, until you learn to solve it.

There is no place to run! No matter where you hide, there will always be yourself and your personal set of problems.

So you can't run away! How do you get out of the mess? Every problem has its solution locked within, but where is the key?

Fortunately you're not in this thing alone. Your faithful friend, the GOD-POWER in you, is always on hand to help. God has no problems; He has only answers. Your own GOD-POWER is infinite. It has all the answers. Get out of the way and let it work for you.

The root cause of all problems is lack of balance, and the solution invariably involves some form of personal growth to right the ship. Be thankful for these challenges which spur your growth. They are the indicators of your areas that are not quite in tune with God's purpose.

Without problems, life gets so dull we invent some. We regularly solve them for pleasure, but we give them slightly different names such as games, puzzles, or contests. We call the more difficult ones marriage, business, religion, and politics, but they all partake of the same essence. We need them because they nudge us toward growth—toward the fulfillment of our purpose on earth. It takes only a little development to solve even your most persistent problems.

Your search for true place starts with a vague but persistent gnawing. Something inside you seems to be eating away at your very being, trying to get you to do something. If only you could figure out what! It must be something important, but how do you get your teeth into it? If you often suffer from this restlessness, rejoice! You don't need a psychiatrist, you need to be about your Father's business. That is your path to peace.

How do you let the GOD-POWER lead you into your true place? By understanding the "rules."

The Lesson of the Present

You are bound in your present situation until you find the truth that frees you. The lesson lies in the path which led you to now. Police your vast motivations to gain more understanding of the thought-feeling-action patterns you used to create your present.

Suppose a Saint suddenly materializes in your living room and spells out exactly how the "Divine Hierarchy" plans for you to be about your Father's business. You are not free to start until you have fulfilled the obligations and digested the lessons of your current situation. Seek your true place by preparing for it. Then when the time comes to move, you will not be retarded by unfinished business.

Those who seek true place as an escape from pressing problems or from drudgery will never find it. It can come only to those who are prepared.

True Place Is a State of Mind

The desire to express the God-Self by serving in your true place is God-given and good. Since this is unquestionably in tune with the Infinite, we are ready to focus the GOD-POWER directly on our problem area. *Now* we must be certain we know exactly what it is we are seeking.

True place is a state of mind. It is the job, family, and station in life you feel is best suited to the special skills and talents you have acquired up to this point. Your own place might not appeal to anybody else on earth, but it will be most desirable to you.

But take care. The more frantically we seek, the more elusive our true place becomes. We job-hop or even marriage-hop, wildly seeking to satisfy that inner gnawing. We are tempted to shrug ourselves off as misfits and drown the yearning and dissatisfaction in "booze," but we know in our hearts that wouldn't work either. We feel trapped on some miserable merry-go-round.

Fortunately there is a way off. Recognize that the wonderful logic factory called your conscious mind isn't capable of finding your true place without help. So resolve to set it aside for the moment. There is an intelligence deep within you which knows what and where your highest good exists. This source of knowledge is the very power we seek to focus on the problem—your own GOD-POWER.

The Hidden Power can and will engineer your date with destiny. Because it is infinite, there is no limit to its operation. It can even be used to focus itself. When we know exactly what we want, we focus the GOD-POWER ourselves, but any time we are in doubt we can use our "automatic focusing apparatus."

How to Achieve Automatic Focusing

The simple name for this complicated focusing device is *faith*. Faith alone can focus and apply the GOD-POWER. Place your problem squarely in its hands by slightly modifying our morning affirmation. Say aloud:

"I trust in God with all my heart, and he directs my growth in the Christ idea. He leads me into my true place, now!"

Use the affirmation aloud when you are alone, or mentally when you are with others. Say it with real feeling and *belief* at least a hundred times a day until you get tangible results.

As you work with this idea, let it change your attitude. Instead of thinking, "I am bored with this job," use the affirmation. Whenever you feel bored or restless, useless or upset, miserable or worried, replace the negative feelings with this positive idea. Fill every little void or dark place with the light of it—"I trust in God with all my heart, and He directs my growth in the Christ Idea. He leads me into my true place, now!"

Live it, eat it, breathe it! Make it part of your very being. As you place your complete trust in the GOD-POWER, there can be no question of an answer. It is the *law of the universe.*

Use God's Suggestions

God gave you a mind, and here is the place to use it. Ideas and opportunity will come to you immediately, but you must be aware enough to recognize them and nimble enough to *use* them constructively.

My writing of this book was brought about by the GOD-POWER in response to just such treatment. The initial prodding was not enough to even remotely suggest a book to me. It was a modest urge to help a handful of struggling souls by present-

ing a few age old ideas in modern language. As the project unfolded within the framework of the original impulsion, it met
with the meager success I expected. From the viewpoint of the
everyday world there were enormous odds against it developing
into anything more. But the GOD-POWER isn't concerned with
the law of averages; it responds according to the deeper laws
of the universe. It unfolded a real joy of expression which was
completely new to me and made what previously looked like
an insurmountable task into a soul fulfilling labor of love.
Meanwhile it effortlessly provided the means of production
and distribution, right on the ideal schedule.

Your Amazing God-Power

Time and again you will be amazed by the uncanny
efficiency of your GOD-POWER. It has a way of pulling together a
bunch of apparently loose ends to weave a tapestry of life you
would never have dreamed possible. The beautiful result often
remains hidden until it bursts forth as a completely accomplished fact.

Your particular background, including all the wonderful and even terrible things you have experienced, makes you
a unique individual with your own unusual mixture of talents
and ability to serve. Somewhere there is a niche where your
special skills and experience can serve better than anyone else
in the world. The omniscient GOD-POWER knows the where-
abouts of your niche. You have but to accept its direction, and
it will lead you to your highest good.

Listen to that little urge within which wants you to perform some tiny but constructive act. If you refuse to take the
first short step, you will never walk to your true place. Stay
alert always—the GOD-POWER may bring your guidance literally
out of the mouth of a babe.

As you continue to use the affirmation, don't be surprised if it suddenly dawns on you that you are already in your true place. Your talents may make you extremely useful to the world right where you are, if you will only use them. This can be a marvelous revelation. But if it should happen to you, take care that you don't lose your desire for further growth.

We must examine the concept of true place in the light of God's over-all evolutionary purpose. How do we reconcile these seemingly conflicting ideas? The answer must be that even true place is not a static situation. We should never allow ourselves to become complacent. Your idea of your true place must be dynamic and susceptible to growth just like every other important thing in life. As you grow, it will either grow with you or you will attract a new one. Never cling to an outgrown true place; it can produce nothing but misery.

One man called himself "the oldest ensign in the navy." During many years in the reserve he refused promotions, hoping to be eligible for discharge as overage. By the time he was called to active duty he was too old to be considered for Lieutenant, J.G. So he spent his whole tour of duty working for lieutenants who were years his junior both in age and experience. Don't do this to yourself!

Continue mentally treating yourself for growth as long as you remain on this earth. Joyously expect that every so often you will grow out of your old true place, right into a new and better one. All life is dynamic in nature; nothing ever stays the same. Growth is the law of the universe. The only real happiness comes from growth through loving service.

Seek the Highest Place

Knowing this, you will seek growth instead of some static form of death you thought was your true place. Growth is the pathway to fulfillment of the wonderful promise of the Master, *"Seek you first the Kingdom of Heaven, and all things will be added unto you."* (Matt. 6:33)

Here we find another paradox. The kingdom of Heaven is within you, as the Master regularly said. But the path to it lies outside the self in loving service. Like all others, this paradox is resolved by a higher truth:

God is infinite being. We understand that His center is everywhere, but His circumference is nowhere. You are created in the image and likeness of God, and in a very real sense your own center is everywhere and circumference nowhere. The path of loving service leads outward everywhere to the center of your being, where resides in regal splendor, the kingdom of Heaven.

Use the Affirmation Method

Sit quietly and recite the affirmation aloud several times, *right now:* "I trust in God with all my heart, and He directs my growth in the Christ Idea. He leads me into my true place, *now!"*

The reason for using any affirmation is to *change* your consciousness. We have regularly stated that your subconscious mind automatically creates circumstances and conditions in your life. These are not random or accidental occurrences, but creations in strict accordance with the basic, immutable laws of the universe. Universal law clearly states that each circumstance or condition coming into your life must conform to a well-developed thought pattern you have allowed to form in your mind. That certainly makes *you* the creator of your own past, present, and future. You create your good and bad by the action of your never sleeping subconscious mind.

But your subconscious is completely dependent upon

your conscious mind for the inputs which develop into thought patterns. Only the thoughts *you choose* to think all day and night long form the patterns which are later reproduced as new circumstances and conditions in your world of experience. You can change *any* area of your life by successfully changing the thought patterns which created it. An affirmation is a good tool with which to produce the change.

Be careful in your choice of affirmations. You must use a statement which doesn't conflict with the logical, reasoning part of your mind. A conflict with your reason causes the logical mind to counter with an opposite thought which is stronger and thus produces negative results. If you do produce negativity, don't blame the technique—correct the affirmation. Make it completely acceptable to your reason; then you will progress.

Substitute the affirmation for your negative thoughts. You don't break a thought pattern by not thinking, but by replacing it with a new one. Sensitize your mind to negative thinking. Ask it to ring an alarm buzzer whenever negativity creeps in.

When you start to think, "I'm stuck in this job with no hope for the future," and the alarm sounds, hit it with the affirmation until it has lost all its punch.

Your Mental Blitzkrieg

Every time your mental alarm bell rings, stop everything and use the affirmation—over and over until you have completely replaced the old thought with the new, positive one. Soon the pattern will be changed. You can tell by the improvement in your daily life.

I call this total saturation use of a good affirmation a *mental blitzkrieg.* That's the way to use it. Wage a large scale lightning war on the thought patterns that are holding you back. Fill your being with the positive until there is absolutely no room for the old pattern. Then keep on using it until it is so firmly established that you are saying and thinking it even in your sleep.

The only way to break a habit is to "erase the old grooves in your head" and replace them with new, stronger ones. Repetition is the stylus. Nothing insures success better than old-fashioned persistence. Call it stubbornness if it amuses you, but stick with it until you win. Remember, victory can only go to the man who gets up one more time than he is knocked down.

Your affirmations should always include growth. Thus you grow ever onward from true place to better true place. Growth is the path to the kingdom of Heaven. With it you will find that *"all things shall be added unto you."* The product of a good affirmation is faith. And, *"According to your faith is it done unto you."* (Matt. 9:29)

True place is yours, *now!*

How to Win Love and Avoid Being Hurt

Let's follow the precious promise of the Master, "Seek, and ye shall find." We seek to understand love. In its purest form, it must be the love expressed directly by God. When you understand how God demonstrates love, you need only learn to do likewise.

chapter eleven

Then you will reap the maximum enjoyment from life's most powerful and rewarding emotion.

In the Bible we find God expressing love: *"For God so loved the world that he gave . . ."* (John 3:16) There is the *secret* of pure love, which leads us to a simple definition: Love is *givingness*. The essence of love is: it *gives of itself and asks nothing in return.*

There is a juvenile type of emotional clinging which many people confuse with love. The Hindus call it "attainment," and go to great lengths in their philosophical writings to teach the value of its opposite, "unattachment." Language and custom differences contribute to confusion, and many Westerners seem to think that the basic teachings of the East are heartless and without love. Nothing could be farther from the truth. Both Hinduism and its cousin, Buddhism, are rich in true love and compassion, though quite dry of childish attachment.

But attachment is the emotion of ownership. It wants to possess and control completely. It wants to be close to its object for better or worse. It is really a thinly disguised form of selfishness. Attachment takes, and so must be the opposite of the givingness which is love. Far from being heartless then, the doctrine of unattachment is a teaching of true personal love.

In direct contrast to attachment, love is selflessness. Love wants the highest good for its object, regardless of personal cost or pain. Love gives freedom, while attachment seeks only to possess.

Attachment is an emotional weakness of young children, but it is surprising how many "adults" have never outgrown it. It appears in more subtle forms in the adult, of course. Where the child might say, "You're my best friend, so I don't want you to play with that nasty old Johnny," the adult will try to disguise the emotion as, "Say, that Johnny sure seems to be a bad influence on you, you're picking up a bunch of his bad habits." Subtle or not, it is still a selfish attempt to enforce your opinion of good or bad upon another. This is the desire to possess and control, masquerading as friendship.

Attachment Can Hurt You

We promised to explain in this chapter why you *cannot be hurt* by someone you really love. Our answer lies in the distinction between love and attachment.

The doting parents wanted their son to become a surgeon. They drilled it into his head from the time he was six years old. But Albert couldn't stand the sight of blood, and the thought of performing an operation almost made him sick. When he quit medical school to become a musician, his parents were deeply hurt.

But it was attachment, not love, that caused it. If you suffer from an emotional clinging you have erroneously called love, you are in trouble. *The object of your attachment can and will hurt you.* It could never be otherwise, since nothing can be completely possessed. There must be periods of separation from anything or anyone, and these will certainly bring pain to one who is deeply attached. Children grow up, husbands go off to work, friends move away—it's inevitable.

To build an attachment and kid yourself that it is love is to sit on an old-fashioned powder keg. It must be blown up on you sooner or later. Carefully examine all your relationships and work to purify them by replacing attachment with love. It will benefit you in many ways while protecting your emotional well-being.

How to Avoid Being Hurt

Because it carries no need to control or possess, *the object of your pure love cannot possibly hurt you.* You desire only what is best for your love-object, regardless of its apparent effect on the immediate personal relationship.

Consider a most extreme case. You have been involved in an affair with a member of the opposite sex. Infatuation has turned to deep love when you discover that your love-object is already married and has a lovely family. You realize that the best thing for this person you love is for you never to see him (or her) again. How would you handle it in your own heart?

Love is givingness. This gift you are impelled to bestow is freedom. You have only to bless the loved one and release him to his highest good. Release him to God. If you have loved, and not possessed, there will be no hurt in it. There will be room in your heart only for happiness in the knowledge that you have given your best for your loved one—that you were not a millstone around his neck or a contributor to what might have been his failure—that you have released him to go on to his highest good.

There is no greater reason to expect absolutes in the love relationship than in any other earthly manifestation. We must accept the practical fact that no relationship on earth is either absolutely pure love or pure attachment. Any intimacy will partake of some of each. No matter how pure your love, it will always contain traces of attachment. So you will occasionally be hurt by a loved one. But now your mental medicine chest is stocked with the world's greatest healing balm.

Whenever you think you have been hurt by a loved one, stop to realize it really wasn't the loved one who did the damage.

Rather the hurt came from your own attachment, from your failure to give. Givingness in love is the healing balm; apply it. Give the necessary forgiveness, understanding, or freedom. You will both receive an increase in growth as a direct result of your givingness.

How to Handle Mishaps of the Heart

You should give a prayer of thanks to your Heavenly Father every time you feel a hurt. It is God's loving gift to you, a reminder that your seemingly perfect love is really quite tarnished by attachment. Love is beautiful and personal, but when it forgets to give and takes instead, it slips into the danger area.

Before we turn to the really wonderful and important aspects of love, let's pause to be sure we are in balance. The Eastern philosophies teach that, by definition, attachment is all bad. But we of the Western world should stick to our belief that nothing is totally bad. Attachment may be a negative manifestation of something, but the something itself must be good. Since attachment is the desire to possess and control its object, we should be able to treat it like any other desire. Let's subject it to the tests of Chapter One: police the motivation.

What is the God-given general desire behind attachment? Isn't it the urge to give to the self? To experience the fulfillment of *being loved?*

Would you call this negative or selfish? The Master said: *"Thou shalt love thy neighbor as thyself."* (Matt. 19:19)

He was clearly calling for balance. You can't give what you don't have. Giving and receiving love are equally important. Therefore a well balanced person will sometimes be called selfish and other times generous.

When you are called selfish for protecting your capacity to give, don't be swayed off balance. The same people criticizing you would gleefully kill the goose that lays the golden eggs. You needn't let them do it to you!

Laying the Foundation for Love

Let's turn our attention to the chapter title, "How to Love and Avoid Being Hurt." The law of attraction and repulsion gives us our key. In order to receive love, you must give it; so we will look first at *how to love.*

You are created in the image and likeness of God. Act like it. Give your love to all of creation; broadcast it daily. This is love's impersonal aspect, but it builds the foundation of general givingness upon which to erect the superstructure of intimate personal relationship.

How to Broadcast Love

How, specifically, shall you broadcast love?

Sit or stand alone and raise your hands with palms facing forward as you would imagine Christ giving a benediction. Then say aloud: "The wonderful light, love, and healing power of God flows forth from me now. It touches, caresses, heals and blesses all mankind and every creature and particle of the universe, bringing to each that which he may need of God's bounty, healing, and love. It also brings to each a more perfect realization of his oneness with God. Heavenly Father, I thank you for the privilege of being a channel for your light and love. Amen."

You will develop your own method and words, but this little prayer is a place to start. The words are not important, it's the *feeling* that counts. *Feel* the light and love actually flowing forth from your hands and heart as you pray that it be so.

Give the universe a treatment of light and love to begin and end each day. Combine it with your morning prayer for personal growth. They blend perfectly, and together their power is amplified.

Build this foundation of impersonal love with tender care. Be sure to include *all* of God's creation. When you no longer wish to withhold it from anyone, you are ready to enter also into the more personal relationship. Your most important experiences grow out of your duplication on the individual, personal level of the same quality of love which God demonstrates on the impersonal, universal level.

The divinity of love of this quality cannot be perceived by the mind. *You must feel it in your heart.* Down through the ages, men have used the *heart* as the symbol of love. This is neither coincidence nor accident.

The Oriental masters taught the truth about the human heart before the dawn of recorded history. It is a major psychic center through which the human organism receives the pure energy of God's love. You use this vital energy in your body, and it is conditioned by all that goes to make up the real you. In turn, you radiate part of it through your heart outward to your personal love objects.

Everyone has experienced some degree of this. When you share a really deep love with someone (or perhaps with a pet animal) you physically feel the sensation in your heart area. As you draw God's wonderful love-energy from the infinite supply around you and direct it to your loved one, you feel it flowing, and your heart seems to expand almost to the bursting point. It creates a bond of love-force that is so vividly felt it has defied description by even the greatest of poets.

What is this love-force? It is God in action! In Chapter

Six we briefly discussed the concept of the Trinity. An elaboration of this will improve our understanding of love-energy.

The true mystical Trinity is symbolized as Father, Mother, and Son. However, the ancient Hebrews considered women to be second class citizens, unfit for direct representation in the Godhead. And since it was these Hebrews who were the founding fathers of Christianity, they managed to confuse the subject by labeling the Mother aspect *Holy Ghost* or *Holy Spirit*.

We want to look at God's love-energy in the act of creation, so we will use the mystic term *Mother* to simplify the study. The aspects of the Trinity are:

1. *Father* may be understood as Light, Intelligence, and therefore Natural Law.

2. *Mother* represents Love, the Creative, the Unformed Potential of substance.

3. *Son* is Power, the Energy of finite substance, Manifestation.

God creates by a simple process analogous to the earthly propagation of mammals. The great universal mind (Father) conceives the idea of an earth or a universe, right down to the most minute detail. This Father Principle then impregnates the Creative (Mother) with the fully developed idea. Such a union of Light and Love creates the finite energy of manifestation which we call Power (Son).

This is true creation, whether it be manifested as a universe or a gnat. And the manifestation will always correspond to the original idea, down to the last detail.

You are created in the image and likeness of God. Therefore you are a miniature trinity of light, love, and power; or intellect, emotion, and physical body. You create in the same manner as God.

How You Create God-Power

You create by duplicating God's simple process. Your intellect (Father) conceives an idea of what you want and works out the details in a mental picture. You impregnate your emotional center (Mother) by dwelling on the mental picture and pouring out love upon it. This union of intellect and emotion induces a flow of creative love-energy which produces the desired manifestation (Son).

In other words, *love causes or creates energy* on the physical plane. That is what you feel in your heart when you consciously love somebody. It is God's love-energy in its purest form, and it is always creative. But to be useful, it must be directed by the intellect, because the manifestation will always be in the image of the creating idea.

How to Utilize the Cardboard Analogy

It is as if the idea were a carefully shaped piece of cardboard which you hold up in front of a light. The shadow it casts is the manifestation, and its shape can only come from the "reality" of the cardboard. Change the shape of the cardboard and you have changed the shadow in exactly the same way; or change the idea and the manifestation changes in strict conformance to the related natural law.

We may thus describe the creative process as: The *idea* held in the *light* of consciousness and bathed in the warmth of *love* calls forth the *energy* that breathes life into the *manifestation*. Thus the Absolute can and does express itself in and as the relative, and we can state:

Every particle of matter is an idea in the mind of God,

made into a physical reality by the energy resulting from a flow of love.

It is love-energy that holds together the nucleus of the atom in the sub-microscopic world; and the same love-energy manifests as the force of gravity in the larger world. Love holds the whole universe together and is the substance of which everything is made.

All this is intensely important to *you* because you can use it practically.

How to Create Your Heart's Desire

Since you are created in the image and likeness of God, you are constantly creating your own world, though largely unconsciously. With this new knowledge you can take charge of the process and use it to create the personal world you really want. You can literally create your heart's desire.

Before you begin the process, carefully police your motivations. Understand exactly what you want and why you want it. Nothing is more disconcerting than to create your "heart's desire," only to discover you didn't want it after all.

Now that you are sure of your heart's desire, examine it in your mind until you are familiar with every detail. Build a perfect mental picture of your desire. Now love this picture! Impregnate your love center with the idea and actually feel the physical love-energy flowing from your heart. Love the idea with the intensity of your full livingness. Mentally direct the flow of your love-energy, and know that it is physically creating your desire. It *is* actually bringing your dream into physical plane manifestation. Then release it with thanksgiving to manifest itself in its own time.

You may experience a miracle that suddenly brings the

manifestation to you full grown, but creation doesn't work that way very often. It normally works by a regulated process of growth. Keep striving to attain your desire, even as you continue to pour out love upon your mental picture.

Let Your Whole Being Become a Magnet

Every time you think about your desire, pour more love upon it and release it to the infinite creative energy. In this way it becomes a law of the universe and *must manifest* itself. By letting the love flow unhampered by any negative emotions, you make your whole being into a huge magnet, attracting all the elements necessary for its rapid manifestation.

Stay alert and maintain an intelligent faith. You will soon encounter a series of happy coincidences or a stroke of good luck out of which will grow, in splendor and magnificence, that which has been your desire. In retrospect you will be amazed at "how lucky you were"; then you will remember that one man's chance is another's certainty. You will know that you *actually worked the natural laws of the universe yourself.*

The ability and power to create, even as He does, is a great gift from our loving Creator. But the second practical use of the creative process is even more wonderful. It is the experience of *being loved.*

The objective is again to insert ourself into the creative process, but this time in reverse. Your life, your very existence, is a direct manifestation of God's love. However, this same life is in all of God's creatures, so we must conclude that it is a simple manifestation of God's *impersonal* love.

But now we seek much more than this. Is it possible to establish and experience a truly *personal* love-relationship with God? We may find the answer in an aviary.

Let's suppose you are a bird fancier and raise parakeets for a hobby. You have several dozen birds in your aviary, all of whom you have raised from the egg. You naturally love all your birds, individually and jointly. But as you might expect of birds living in a large aviary, they pay very little attention to you. This in itself is a mark of affection between you and the birds because they become frightened and agitated when any stranger comes near. This situation is quite like the relationship between God and the bulk of His human creations. We can call this a general, impersonal love.

Now, if one of these birds began to show a special interest in you, wouldn't you respond? What if one parakeet began to fly right to you every time you entered the aviary? He regularly perches on your shoulder as you go around filling feeders, changing water, cleaning, and performing the many enjoyable little tasks of bird care. All the while, this little feathered friend nuzzles you and says, "I love you, my wonderful caretaker. Thank you for your loving, tender care. But most of all, thank you for the privilege of your companionship."

Wouldn't your relationship with this particular bird change? You wouldn't love your other birds any less. And you would still give them your same loving care. But you would find a new friendship growing between you and that specially loving bird. Certainly you would respond to his little plea and enter into a truly *personal* relationship with him. He would become something special to you, and you would quite naturally give him more personal care and attention.

Your special friend's extra care would not in any way lessen the status or take something away from the other birds. In fact, it might well increase your interest in everything connected with the aviary. None of the birds have lost anything;

the only difference is the enrichment of your life and that of your special parakeet by the new relationship.

This homely example falls far short of pointing out the depth and richness of the potential experience, but it should serve as a convincing argument to your mind. You know *your* heart is not so cold as to refuse response to that little parakeet. And if you, who are on earth, feel that response in your heart, how much more wonderful must be the response of Infinite Love to the appeal of one of Its humans?

This is the very relationship you can build with God. Why do *you* have to be the one to build it? Why doesn't God? Let's go back to our example. You, as the caretaker, regularly shower your blessings upon all your birds. Often you stop and try to give a little personal affection to some individual, but you are generally completely ignored. You would love to give more affection; you may ache for more companionship with your birds, but you can only give what they are willing to accept. The special parakeet who regularly flies to your shoulder wants to accept more from you, so you give gladly. Both you and the bird are enriched in the process. And so it can be between you and God.

You have a big advantage over the parakeet. You don't have to wait for your Caretaker to come into your aviary. You can talk to God anytime, anywhere, silently or out loud. The main thing is, do it! Talk to God just like you were the little parakeet. Say:

> Most wonderful Father-Mother God, I thank you with all my heart for your gift of life and the countless blessings you regularly bestow on me. Thank you for your tender, loving care. I love you, heavenly Father-Mother. I try to reflect back to you, in my own small way, some portion of the wonderful love you have given me in your gift

of life. Please commune with me now. Let me partake of the
added blessing of your *personal love.*

When you dwell on the ideas of this short prayer, you
are truly greeting God as He enters your aviary. Just as quickly
as you would respond to the little parakeet, God *will* answer
you. Use the invocative: *"Let me* partake of the added blessing
of your *personal love."*

It has been said in all religions and all languages, "As
you turn to God, God turns to you." This is God's own promise
of response, and *it will not be broken.* It will suit itself to your
temperament and beliefs. God will answer you in the exact
terms of your deepest inner conception of the mystic experience.

You may feel a gentle tingling sensation that seems to
say, "I am here, my beloved." Or you may experience the
tongues of living flame which leave you a completely new individual, full of the fire of the Holy Spirit. Or you may have a
totally unique and privately personal experience. But no matter
what it is, you will receive a personal response from God.
Try it!

If there seems to be no immediate response, look inside
yourself. Have you policed your motivations for seeking this
experience? Are you sincere? Did you get off alone, away from
the pressures of everyday life, before you tried to reach God?
Were you relaxed? Did you eliminate all fear and doubt? Do
you really think you are worthy of a response from God?

When you can answer yes to all those questions, you
have your response from God. Most often the block lies in the
question, "Do you really think you are worthy of a response
from God?" That doubt is a leak bigger than the whole hose.
Get rid of it now! Remember the little parakeet. Was it worthy
of a response from you? It was more than worthy, and you felt
your life enriched by the new relationship!

And so it is between God and you. You will *both* be enriched by the beauty of this new relationship.

Choose to enter into this personal relationship with God, now! Do your part. Seek! And God will, yea *must*, respond. Then in the highest sense, you will love and be loved.

You will dwell in the "secret place of the Most High," under His personal protection. He *will* anoint your head with the oil of joy! Surely goodness and mercy will follow you all the days of your life, and you *will* dwell in the House of the Lord, forever.

▲ How to Free Yourself from Earthly Cares

Our purpose now is to pick up the threads of thought from the preceding chapters and weave them into a meaningful tapestry. We have emphasized many inter-relations between the various facets of life as we traveled on our journey around the double spiral. Now we

chapter twelve
▼

seek a broad concept of life as a whole that will lend new meaning to its many bits and pieces.

As we search together, we must avoid thinking of firm lines between the material, the mental, and the spiritual worlds. There is only *one world* with material, mental, and spiritual aspects. We find this understanding in many religions, embodied in some variation of the Trinity. At the center of the Trinity is the Unity—one God, but with three aspects. We have studied these as Father (Spirit—Intellect), Mother (Love—the Universal Subconscious), and Son (Manifestation—the Material World).

Beware of compartmentalized thinking. Understand, now and forever, the Trinity is *one*, life is *one*, and *you are one*. There is no neat separation in real life. The lines between the principles of the Trinity are fuzzy, as are the lines between acquaintance and friend or like and love. The intellect of the Father aspect shades subtly into the receptive, creative mind of the Mother Principle. Then it appears as the Infinite Love which we generally consider to be the center of the Mother aspect. And manifestation, or the Son Principle, flows so smoothly out of the Mother that there simply isn't a place where one stops and the other starts. These things are true whether we are speaking of the Trinity which is God or the trinity which is you. By following this reasoning we can reach a deeper understanding from the statement that man is created in the "image and likeness of God."

Why You Must Act Like God

Since man *is* the image and likeness of God, we can logically deduce that his *reason for being* is to express in the finite world those same attributes which God expresses in the vastness of His infinite universe. In simple words, you were put here to *act like a god.* Naturally the higher elements of your inner self know this already. Only the relatively tiny lower part of you thinks it is just a physical body governed by a grey cellular mass called a brain. This same lesser part naturally thinks it is the brain which needs to be educated, rather than the lower self.

But it is the education of the lesser self to an understanding of its proper role in the Universe which constitutes the process called *growth.* Therefore in Chapter One we stated that *your reason for being* is growth. In the everyday world that is the whole truth. But now it is time to look for a longer range goal—a final culmination of your growth process on earth.

Let's follow our tested course and look again at nature for our clue. From the tiniest single-celled creature or plant all the way to the most complex organism walking the earth, we see evolution in progress. Man has rightly studied nature. And by gaining an understanding of certain principles of evolution, he has been able to "create" new and better varieties of plant and animal life to increase his food supply and generally make his material life easier.

Look anywhere and everywhere. Each form of life is steadily evolving toward a higher and more complex expression. This is true in more than just the purely material sense. There is certainly evolution of consciousness! A brief consideration of that process should begin to shed real light on the question of our ultimate goal.

Evolution Governs Your
Ultimate Growth

Plants exhibit a rudimentary form of consciousness. Modern electrical instruments have definitely shown that a tomato will register a form of pain and anxiety when cut or punctured. All green plants seek light by some means or another. The most obvious example is the sunflower. It senses the direction of the sun and turns to face it, turning throughout the day to keep its face constantly pointed toward the source of life-giving light.

As we travel up the scale, animals demonstrate increasing degrees of consciousness and intelligence until we find some dogs, monkeys, and porpoises which we call almost human. Perhaps human consciousness can aspire to heights which are as far above the human of today as the human is above the sunflower. But our practical approach must still seek a goal near enough to be attained in one or two lifetimes.

Let's look deeper into the evolutionary process in search of a reasonable goal. In all the complex scheme of life we find nature constantly re-using the same materials. What is waste or death to one form of life is sustenance to another. The herbivorous animals are food for the carnivores. The excretions, and even the bodily remains of each, return to the soil to nourish another generation of plant life. The cycle is so perfect it staggers the imagination. Even the process of breathing by animals fits the pattern. It supplies the vegetable world the carbon dioxide needed to build its physical substance, while this very building by the plants liberates the oxygen so necessary to the animals.

In one sense nature is lavish and abundant, producing beauty in the profusion of flowers and greenery which add a whole dimension of meaning to human life. But in another very real sense, nature is completely frugal. For instance, she stored up the vegetation of countless centuries in the form of the coal and oil which power our present day civilization. Nothing is ever lost to the natural world. Its form may be changed, but the inherent energy of it remains somewhere waiting for another use.

Even in the light of atomic fission, fusion, and nuclear explosions, the frugality of nature remains true. We have only to accept the concept of a continuum between the building blocks or atoms and the basic elemental energy from which they are formed. Our modern chemists and physicists would express this as a law: Matter-energy can neither be created nor destroyed, but it may be changed from one form to another. This basic law of physics-chemistry will lead us to the goal we seek.

If God (or nature) is so careful of His atoms and energies which are relatively inert and deed, isn't it reasonable to deduce that He is equally frugal with this precious commodity we call consciousness? We can look upon consciousness as a higher expression of the matter-energy continuum and begin to embrace the concept of the conservation of consciousness.

Free Yourself from Earthly Consciousness

The basic laws of nature are uniform in their application regardless of the magnitude of the manifestation. So said Hermes centuries ago, "As above, so below." We should be able to apply the law of conservation of matter-energy by simply restating it as the law of conservation of consciousness:

Consciousness can neither be created nor destroyed, but it may be changed from one form to another.

We will be half-way through the next chapter before we can fully expound on this law, but we still absorb enough now to understand the nature of our goal.

In matter-energy it is the smallest independent particle, the atom, which enjoys nature's most complete protection. Similarly, we would expect this protection for the smallest independent unit of consciousness. Now this smallest unit must be the consciousness of an individual. It is for reasons such as these that over two-thirds of the earth's population accept some form of the concept or doctrine known as *reincarnation*.

What Reincarnation Means to You

Reincarnation is a simple exposition of the law of conservation of consciousness. It asserts that at the transition called the "death" of your physical body, the real "you" (your own highly evolved consciousness) is changed in form, but not destroyed. Your precious consciousness undergoes a cycle of rest and perhaps education on other planes. Then you return to earthly manifestation in a new body, taking up where you left off to continue your personal evolutionary process.

You enter the new born baby body as its life with its first independent breath. The type of body and the total of the environmental circumstances are exactly what you have earned by the sum of your thoughts and actions in all of your previous lives. Each successive life (or incarnation) builds upon the lessons and heritage of all those past.

What a relief this concept of reincarnation can be to the inquiring mind! Here at last is a logical explanation of the justice of unequal birth—material, physical, financial, mental, spiritual, and all the rest. Each person gets the start in this life which is exactly equal to what he has earned by the sum of all his past lives.

So some people are orphaned, blind, crippled, or poor! This no longer looks like the caprice of some Oriental despot men call God. Instead it reveals the perfect functioning of natural law, the inexorable balancing of the scales of justice. It even makes sense out of that dreadful passage of Exodus:

". . . *visiting the iniquity of the fathers upon the chil-dren, and upon the children's children, unto the third and to the fourth generation.*" (Exod. 34:7)

Now we can understand it as the normal operation of the law of attraction. Like attracts like. A soul coming into in-carnation will naturally be attracted into a family with the morals and approach to life most like itself. And so it really happens that the iniquity of the father attracts like children into the family, unto the third and fourth generation. But there is a wonderful flip side to the coin. You can also attract highly evolved souls into your family by creating a home atmosphere of goodness, truth, and beauty.

The Practical Value of Reincarnation

Just what is the real and practical value of this teaching? It is the paradox that knowledge of lives past and of others to come gives meaning and importance to this one. *This life* is important not just for itself, but also for the effect it will have on all your future incarnations.

It clearly demonstrates the futility of suicide. You can't escape anything that way; you merely build yourself a tougher set of problems to face next time. If you make too big a mess out of this life, you may earn a pretty miserable start in the next one, and on and on. But a life well-lived is another mile-stone on the long path to your ultimate goal.

Before beginning the discussion of the goal itself, let's answer one question that invariably enters your mind when it is first exposed to reincarnation. That is: "If I have lived all those other lives, why can't I remember any of them?"

The answer is simplicity itself. Most people today couldn't stand the knowledge. It would literally destroy them. The average memory is bad enough anyway. How much can you remember of the first six years of this life? Or even of last year? Why should you be further confused with memories left over from a hundred previous incarnations. We are many times better off without the knowledge of all the terrible stunts we probably pulled while struggling along the lower rungs of the ladder of evolution.

Our Creator, in His infinite wisdom, has fixed it so that we are cut off from memory of the past just as we enter our new body. If this were not true, imagine the utter frustration of a fully mature adult mind with complete memory of all its past activities, imprisoned in the totally uncoordinated six or eight pounds of a brand new infant body. It would be driven crazy before it had lived more than a few hours.

Give thanks to our loving God that you are not burdened with the memory of past lives until you have evolved to the point where the information will be of practical value to you. Know that there is a point in your personal progression where you will gain the strength and courage necessary to cope with this knowledge. When you have grown to that place, earned the revelation, and need it, it will be given to you. Then you will have *conclusively proved eternal life* to yourself. And it matters not whether you can get it across to someone else.

We can consider personal knowledge of your past lives part of the ultimate goal. It ties in with the concept of continuity of consciousness which we will develop in the next chapter, but we want a look at our goal first. Let's stop now and build a clear picture of it—the purpose of this life and all your other lives, past or future.

How to Understand the Goal
of Your Life

Look upon one incarnation as a day, or perhaps a semester, of school. The ultimate goal of this and each succeeding life is to grow in knowledge and wisdom—to finally achieve such complete mastery over the things of this world that you have no further need to return to another body. In other words, the object is to "graduate" from the school of earth life—or is it?

As with the schools of men, the real importance is not the ceremony of graduation or the diploma. Rather, it is the change wrought in the individual. It is his growth, the wisdom acquired from the whole of the study process, and the disciplines developed along the way. Let's compromise and call our goal the fruition or culmination of the entire process of successive incarnation, symbolized by a "graduation exercise."

As in man made schools, a better word than graduation would be commencement. You do commence a new and far more wonderful life with this event. Let's float away from the practical for just a moment to speculate on what that new life might be. After commencement, what?

In the manner of earthly colleges, some graduates choose to stay behind and teach. They advance their own growth process by giving in the great effort to improve mankind by helping their younger brothers along the pathway of learning.

Many other graduates feel tired of the academic way, and their urge for growth leads them to strike out and seek their fortune. Both groups are right. The choice is a personal one and must suit the individual's aptitudes and inclinations. The important point is the opportunity to exercise your free choice at the end of the current evolutionary process.

"Graduation" is just one more milestone on the path of evolution. When this goal is attained another will appear, far more wonderful than the first—and on and on, from glory to glory. The spiral of life is endless. There are worlds and states of consciousness beyond our finite understanding. To contemplate this vastness of wonder, order, growth, beauty, symmetry, and perfection is staggering to the imagination, but enlightening to the soul. Enjoy it for a moment, then we will steer our little pink cloud back down to earth.

How to Work Toward
Your Goal

We have looked for an ultimate goal and discovered it is beyond the reach of our finite understanding. However, we did outline an objective suitable for the rest of this incarnation. It arises out of the logical question, "How can I best work toward graduation from this school of earth life?"

Our answer lies in the details of the school analogy. How do you best work toward graduation from any school? It is necessary to plan a sequence of courses which meets the requirements of your college and thereby fits you for usefulness in the world beyond. You must major in something, but also acquire knowledge and proficiency in a wide variety of subjects to give you depth, polish, and a real awareness of the world around you.

Planning the course is but a small fraction of the work and study necessary to the over-all accomplishment. You must enroll in one group of classes at a time, then experience and live each class meeting and keep up with the assigned research and homework. There are no shortcuts to a well rounded education. It's like walking around the block; it has to be done *one step at a time.*

In a book such as this, we can suggest a general course

of study. But only *you* can live it! Only you can provide the impetus and interest that make the difference between Phi Beta Kappa and failure. However there is no escape in failure. You can't flunk out of the school of life. The only exit is at the top—graduation! So how shall you start?

First, understand that your higher self has all knowledge of your past lives, including all your achievements and failures. It has already planned the basic lessons for this incarnation, much like a loving parent picks a school most suited to his young child's needs and aptitudes. Your exact position at any given point in this life is the direct result of your success or failure in learning your assigned lessons. And your future comfort and happiness depend upon your success or failure in learning today's lessons.

How to Join Forces With Your Higher Self

To really enjoy life you must join forces with your higher self. Your conscious effort to cooperate evokes response in accordance with our friendly old maxim, "As you turn to God, God turns to you."

Your higher self is nothing less than God's personal ambassador to you, and its response is always immediate and complete. We have each felt God's response in our parakeet analogy. If the Infinite itself never fails to respond to your plea, how willing and eager must be that particular part of It which is your own higher self!

One interesting way to approach your higher self is to consider it a separate entity and give it a name. Talk to it. Say something like, "Hi, George, I realize it's time we were getting better acquainted. I want to accept your guidance and help in learning the lessons of this incarnation, so please start transmitting." Then form a definite habit of stopping whenever you have a doubt about something. Ask, "Hey, George, what do you think about this?"

Why the Higher Self
Must Respond

Have no doubt about this! If you are sincere, "George" will give you a straight answer every time. You can use "him" as a second conscience, a father confessor, a friend, and a true inspiration. He will never be too busy to help, and he will never let you down. In the next chapter we will discover that each of us has many unseen helpers, but of all of them, your own "George" is the most important. He is your personal link to the Infinite and to eternal life. As you make the effort to get acquainted with him, you will experience an acceleration of your whole growth pattern.

Christ gave us the promise: *"Ask and you shall receive."* Your very act of asking grants "George" permission to send help from the higher planes of life. Ask him to help you identify with God's great plan for the universe.

Listen for his guidance as you seek to tread the pathway of evolution with enthusiasm balanced by patience, with love balanced by wisdom, and with the pure white light of the Christ Consciousness ever growing in your heart.

Make no mistake about it! The light is *real!* It has been seen, felt, and experienced by the enlightened mystics of all ages. Ask "George" to help you find it. Pray to God any way that appeals to you, but be sure you pray for the light. *The light is real!* It is reality itself. When you sense its first faint glimmerings, follow it faithfully. It is the *certain path* to God.

You may question the practicality of seeking God. Why should you bother? After all, you can use the practical tech-

niques of the first twelve chapters to create a pleasant and prosperous life *here and now*. So why chase off after this will-o'-the-
wisp called God? No words can suffice for your answer; it must
come as a *personal experience*. Your first tiny glimpse of the
light will give you more reason than a hundred million words.

You only speculate upon the truths of life until your
seeking brings the first glimmer. But when you are still, and the
light comes, you are changed forever.

Just as Jacob wrestled with his angel, so you can wrestle
with your own "George." And as surely as Jacob received his
blessing, so will you. But there is the inevitable price to pay.
The Bible says the angel touched Jacob's thigh and thereafter
he walked with a limp. That seems a terrible price for any
blessing, until you understand the allegory. The meaning of
the limp is simply that Jacob was changed so completely it
noticeably affected his approach to life (symbolized as his way
of walking).

As you wrestle with "George," your approach to life
will be changed. The difference may be so great that some of
your grosser friends would call you a "double-barreled square."
To them you might appear to be "walking with a limp," but in
reality they are the ones who are out of step with the universe.
Learn to walk the path of life arm in arm with your own wonderful "George." You will unfold talents and a degree of livingness you never dreamed were within your reach. You will *seek*
and *find* the light.

Use a New Name and a
New Nature

Then, we are told, Jacob was given a new name. In Bible
allegory a name refers to the nature of the thing. So a new name
means that Jacob was given a new nature. The name became

Israel, which means *wholeness.* Indeed Jacob did become a whole-being as a result of his experience. It will happen to you when *you experience the light.*

> And he said, Thy name shall be called no more Jacob, but Israel: for as a prince hast thou power with God and with men and hast prevailed. And Jacob asked him and said, Tell me, I pray thee, thy name. And he said, Wherefore is it that thou dost ask after my name? And he blessed him there. *(Gen. 32:28-29)*

The angel didn't give his name, but we have already named him. He is your own "George."

> And Jacob called the name of the place Peniel: for I have seen God face to face, and my life is preserved. *(Gen. 32:30)*

As you seek, you will find the place Jacob called Peniel is your own pineal body or pineal gland. You will reach up to "George" through the gateway of the pineal and experience God face to face. Once you have "seen" God, your life is "preserved" because *you actually own eternal life.* You will live in the *light* and experience at will the peace that passeth all understanding.

Now is the appropriate time. Seek the *light!*

▲
How
to Live
in the Light

Each of us must find and walk the path of light before being relieved of the requirement for future incarnations. We may not finish our work during the remainder of this lifetime, but progress will certainly make our future struggles easier. Good, practical

chapter thirteen

▼

growth comes from the simple act of seeking. That which you seek is the essence of your true reason for existence. It is another aspect of the kingdom of Heaven.

How shall we seek this *light?* Would that there were a simple formula like our Formula For Personal Creation, but this time it isn't that easy. We can only outline a broad, general approach. From there you are on your own. You must work out the details for yourself, but that is as it should be.

How to Find Your Path of Light

To begin the discussion, let's go back to some basic truths. In these materialistic times, most of us have been taught that the only realities of life are those which we are able to experience by means of one or a combination of our five senses, namely sight, hearing, touch, taste, and smell. There have always been men with the knowledge that there is more to life than just the senses, but they are a very small minority. However it is the work of this minority which leads us to the first faint traces of the path of light.

This minority of scientists, scholars, religionists, and assorted screwballs works in the broad field now called extrasensory perception. ESP is simply a term used to describe those faculties of man and animals which cannot be directly attributed to the five "objective" senses.

Some examples of ESP in animals are: the navigational ability of the homing pigeon; the ability of the salmon to find its way back to the place of its birth to spawn; the ability to "read the calendar" exhibited by the swallows who come back to Capistrano; and the dog or cat that finds his family although they have moved many miles away. You can undoubtedly add many more from your personal experience.

In this century our scientists have begun to seriously

study ESP in animals and man. For instance, Dr. J. B. Rhine's work at Duke University is well known to most of the literate inhabitants of the Western world. To any who may have missed Dr. Rhine's book, *The Reach of The Mind*,[1] do read it. It is a classic in this field. Then read others. Let your imagination be piqued by a good survey of the scientific knowledge and approach to ESP. It won't take much effort, and the increase in your perceptive abilities that results may amaze you.

What Is ESP?

ESP seems to be an extension of the physical senses by some unknown power or substance. There are many variations or aspects, and man has named them in terms related to the physical senses. The extension of sight is called clairvoyance; of hearing, clairaudience; and of touch, clairsentience. Other manifestations not as directly related to one physical sense are called intuition, telepathy, psychokinesis, precognition, psychometry, and the like.

Every individual, *including you*, has some degree of ESP and the potential to develop more. No two people will unfold the same aspect at the same rate, because of the tremendous variations of aptitude. But there is definitely some potential in every human being. You will find it fun and beneficial to discover your own.

How to Discover and Develop Your ESP

There are any number of exercises or games you can play with yourself to discover and develop your promising areas of ESP. In each exercise you will find that your results improve

---

[1] Wm. Sloane Assoc., Inc., New York, 1947.

when you are relaxed and accept the *very first* fleeting thought or impression that comes to you.

Here are a few simple, but effective exercises:

1. When your telephone rings, stop for a split second before answering it and ask yourself who is calling. Keep a little log, recording each call and noting who you thought it was and who it actually turned out to be. Notice how your accuracy improves from week to week as you learn to accept that first impression. You may begin to pick up a mental picture of the person calling and so develop your clairvoyance; you may get it clairaudiently or intuitively. The mechanics are not significant, but your improving accuracy may open the door for your first good look at the unseen side of life.

2. Duplicate game # 1 with your doorbell.

3. Think of a friend and mentally send him a request to call you on the phone (or write you a letter). Prepare your mental request carefully and write down the date, time, and the friend's name. Then release it and temporarily forget it. Record your results. Even if your friend doesn't answer your mental call, he may have received your thought, but somewhere where he couldn't respond. Ask about it without giving away your reason. Watch your successes to see how your proficiency improves from week to week.

4. Sit quietly near a friend or acquaintance and be receptive to his thoughts. Anticipate what he is about to say and say it with him. Or offer him the drink of water he was about to ask for. This exercise is for your telepathic receptivity, just as # 3 was for your sending ability.

5. Hold an object such as a watch or ring belonging to an acquaintance and ask it how he feels. If you are receptive you will feel his physical symptoms as if they were your own.

Then ask it what is his dominate desire at the moment. Again, you should feel it momentarily as your own. When you get results with this, you are practicing the art of psychometry.

The Practical Value of ESP

"Games" like these will help you recognize and develop the different aspects of your ESP. But understand that, like the Trinity, ESP is *one*. We study it by analyzing its aspects, but there is serious error if you let your thinking remain compartmentalized. It matters not which of the forms you use to gain information or results, as long as it works!

Most people fail to use their extrasensory powers simply because they don't realize they have them. It will pay you to discover yours for two practical reasons. First it will increase your awareness of the world around you, thus increasing your efficiency in the affairs of everyday living. And second, it will provide a means of direct communication with the unseen world. The deep importance of this will become more apparent as we unfold a new set of concepts.

As we would expect, the line between the five senses and ESP is not neat and clear. There are many places where one shades into the other. For instance, there is a bridge between ESP and common eyesight. During World War II the Air Force made extensive use of the human faculty called night vision. It is a scientific fact that we use a different set of nerve endings in the eye to see in bright light than we use in near-darkness. Night vision nerves are slightly offset from our day vision nerves. Consequently night vision is effective when you look at an object obliquely (almost like looking out of the corner of your eye), while regular day vision works best when you look directly at the objects.

By using a mirror and the simple principle of night vision, many people are able to discover the existence of a manifestation of the vital life force called the human aura. The part of the aura normally observed this way is a white or pastel colored light which surrounds the entire body but is most easily distinguished about the head.

Let's try to see your aura now. Sit before a mirror in soft light, bordering on semi-darkness. Applying the principle of night vision, stare at the point approximating the center of your forehead, but *look* at the area immediately surrounding your head just above the hair. If you keep from blinking you will very shortly see that your head is actually surrounded by a filmy, but definite, light. You may get the sensation of color, or it may appear as a plain white light. But *light* it is!

With a little practice you will become proficient enough to see your aura after just a second or so. Next, use the same technique to see the aura around your fingers. A solid background, preferably white, replaces the mirror for this. When you see their auras easily, bring your two hands almost together with the fingers pointing at each other. Notice how the force-field forms and flows between them. When you feel familiar with your aura, start looking for auras around your friends. Now that you know what you are looking for, it will be easy.

Don't be surprised when you find assorted colors, sizes, and shapes of auras on different people. Infinite degrees of livingness and thought manifest themselves in the human aura, and you may see all or merely a part of each different one. Take care not to pass judgment on the development or well-being of the person observed. A whole science of aura must be mastered before you could presume to do something like that.

Practical Value of Seeing
the Aura

What is this aura we see, and what good is the ability to see it? It is your link to the unseen world which is truly *the world of reality*. Everything that exists in the three dimensional world has an aura. It must come into existence in the real world of light before it is born into this shadow world of manifestation. We are enslaved by the shadows we falsely label reality, until we learn this truth. That is the meaning of those wonderful words of the Master, *"You shall know the truth, and the truth shall set you free."* (John 8:32)

What good to see it? It confirms to your lower self the truth of the higher existence. The aura is *light,* and that light is the essence of your very livingness. To obtain more light is to increase the degree or quality of your livingness. It is a product of conscious evolution.

Examine your aura every morning as you brush your teeth. There you will see the living evidence of the state of your health and spiritual progress. It takes only a short time to recognize and understand the changes. Look well and take heed of the practical lessons to be derived from this report card.

Auras are pure light. As you become accustomed to observing them, you will often notice one or two which seem not to belong to anything or anybody. Don't be confused by this. They are real, too. You have then seen your first discarnate entity, or spirit, if you prefer the term.

Some good evidence of existence after we surrender our physical bodies is the regular observation of the auras of individuals in the discarnate (or disembodied) state. When your

ESP is developed enough, you can "talk" to them yourself and prove again that "death" is only the gateway to something more.

Understanding Spirit Photography

Some people often "catch" spirits on film, that is, they photograph discarnate entities. I must confess only limited success with the spirit photography I attempted while writing this book. However I was blessed with a few interesting manifestations in spite of my basic ignorance of the general field of photography.

Why should a grown man try to catch a spirit on film? Let's postpone that to our concluding chapter and turn instead to the next concept in our study of discarnate entities.

How to Communicate with
a Teacher

The idea of communication with the spirit world seems of little practical value if we confine our thinking to "talking" with just any old spirit who wanders by. I personally resisted the idea for several years, but not because I believed it impossible. I just couldn't see any good to be derived from an exchange of greetings with our dear departed Aunt Minnie, lovable though she may be.

However my attitude changed completely when I encountered the concept of a Spiritual Teacher. Here is a *reason* to communicate with the world beyond. It is entirely possible to learn things not yet discovered by our hard working scholars and scientists. In fact, there might be a whole new frontier for science and scholarship, but there is a tremendous hurdle involved in trying to objectively measure an essentially subjective manifestation. Can it be accomplished in our generation? Permit me to defer this also to our concluding chapter.

How to Contact Your Teacher

Can *you* discover and personally communicate with a Spiritual Teacher? As far back as men can remember, great minds have nurtured the idea of an angelic being who watches over the personal destiny of each individual. In the Western world this wonderful guide and protector is most often called a "Guardian Angel," while in the Orient he is more apt to be called simply a Spiritual Teacher.

Each individual is assigned a guardian angel or teacher before birth. This one spirit remains with you for the entire course of an incarnation. There may be other spirits who work with you along the way, but this one teacher is permanent.

We have now set forth the two most important beings you will encounter in your whole lifetime. First is your own higher self whom we nicknamed "George," and next is your permanent guardian angel or spiritual teacher. The very positive value of developing your faculties of ESP reveals itself as we cast about for a means of direct communication with these amazingly positive influences.

Since "George" and your Teacher have no tangible physical bodies, the only possible means of directly talking to them must be some form of ESP. As you continue your ESP exercises and find areas of effectiveness, you are building the means of intercourse with them. What is the practical value of direct personal communication with your Teacher? It will be somewhat different for each one of us.

In my own case the contact is based on an aspect of ESP best described as a combination of clairsentience and intuition. It has two distinct practical values for me. First it is a constant source of personal guidance and inspiration. It has helped bail me out of some pretty sticky situations, and it regularly leads me into richly rewarding experiences. Second, it is a bottomless well of material, instantly available to see me through speaking engagements, personal consultations, or spiritual writing. It is even a help with the little things. It will help find your misplaced watch, or locate a new job if you ask for it.

Certainly this book is a result of communication with my Teacher. The wonderful part is, I learned more by writing it than anyone could possibly learn from reading the finished product.

Like so many of our step by step examples, a book must be written one word and one sentence at a time. But at any given point I can't tell whether it is really me or my unseen helpers performing the task. Sometimes the typewriter goes at a rate I know is two or three times faster than I can type myself. In fact, I wrote the first few chapters in longhand for my secretary to decipher, and then bought a typewriter almost against my better judgment. I was afraid I couldn't type and think at the same time, because I hadn't looked at a typewriter since high school.

But a strange thing happened. The work progressed much faster than before. The conclusion I suggest is that one of my unseen helpers was an excellent typist in her last incarnation.

The Practical Value of Spirit Assistance

How can a person objectively value such help? Again I ask you to let me give my sincere answer in the final chapter. But let's agree on the pragmatic answer right here.

Assume for a moment this idea of unseen help is "all in my head." What difference does it make so long as it provides the inspiration and courage to try? It is only as we are inspired to *try* that we put ourselves in a position to accomplish something. And it follows that anything which inspires us to try is good—even though our trying may result in temporary failure. No matter that you sometimes fail. You learn as much from failure as from success, and it is the learning that fulfills the purpose of your incarnation.

Work to Contact Your
Spiritual Teacher

Somewhere along your path of lives *you* must learn to *consciously* cooperate with the great evolutionary plan of the Universe. As long as you remain out of touch with the guidance and help that is always available from your teachers, you will operate at a distinct disadvantage. A very real part of cooperation with the evolutionary force is contact with those whose vision is not restricted by the confines of mortal flesh.

Unfortunately no one can give you a foolproof formula for this form of contact. And it is not the sort of phenomenon readily demonstrable in the laboratory. But it is *possible,* and you owe it to yourself to develop a system that will work for you. Work on your ESP exercises and pray for contact. You will be answered.

There are individuals and organizations who advertise they can bring you personal spirit contact or even "Mastership" in a few short mail order lessons. It isn't that easy! If anyone guarantees you specific results in a specified time, don't waste your effort or money. A *guarantee* is a sure sign of fraud, though the guarantor may be sincere and just too naïve to know better.

Also there are truly dedicated "mediums" who conduct "unfoldment classes" for sincere seekers. It is possible to get real help from some of these classes. However, much depends upon the way your personality blends with the inevitable prejudice and mental blind spots of the particular medium you work with. I don't believe I have ever contacted an insincere medium, but in a field such as this, sincerity alone is hardly enough. They all demonstrate some degree of ESP, but a little bit of knowledge or ability turned loose on the public with a touch of showmanship can be downright dangerous. Mediums might be compared in this respect to medical doctors. There are good ones and those who are not so good. And even the best ones don't have all the answers. Know your doctor or your medium before you put all your trust in him.

It is important to seek contact with our unseen guardians and helpers. We are destined to cooperate with them if we would continue to grow. But it is essential that you balance and control your seeking with a well-disciplined intellect. There are absolutely no shortcuts! Growth is a steady process which can't be by-passed, but of course it can be aided. The tools are balance and discipline.

Yes, it is possible for humans living in bodies of flesh to contact the unseen world and communicate with its inhabitants. But we must not go overboard! We still live in *this world* of apparently three space and one time dimensions. Here we must live, work, and learn our lessons. We need to satisfy the requirements of this world to earn the privilege of fellowship and help from the unseen. The underlying thought ties in well with the very old saying, "The Lord helps those who help themselves."

How to Handle Your New Responsibilities

It is always necessary to stand on your own two feet. When *you* have put forth the effort to learn how the process works, you will be able to communicate with your spiritual teacher. However, this is not a panacea or a release from all responsibility. If anything, contact with a guardian angel will increase your responsibility because you no longer have the excuse of ignorance. If it only tends to complicate matters, why bother? In any one incarnation, that is your personal choice. But you must contact and work with the unseen world before you can graduate from the school of earthly existence.

Some individuals hesitate to finish school. They find all kinds of interesting courses and become known as perennial seniors. Similarly, it's your privilege to waste an incarnation or two if you feel like it. But sooner or later you must take the required courses and graduate. Why not start now?

Some may question the necessity of the unseen teacher in the school of life, but none would doubt the requirement for professors in a college. The situations are sufficiently similar that there is no problem of understanding. A student, no matter how brilliant, just isn't qualified to grub out a well-rounded education without guidance and instruction. And this help can best come from those who have traveled the pathway of learning far enough to have earned the title, Teacher.

A good teacher instinctively sets up learning situations well-suited to the individual student's needs. He has the perspective and breadth of knowledge which can save the pupil years of wasted effort, but he still allows the little mistakes which are such an important part of the learning process. There is *no* substitute for a good teacher.

Why haven't we set down a simple way to meet and talk to your teacher? The most straightforward answer is another old saying from the occult lore: "When the pupil is ready, the Master appears." This is not begging the question! It's a simple statement of fact, no different from the setting forth of college entrance requirements. You must *earn* the right to enter a col-

lege by acquiring the prescribed knowledge and mental disciplines. In the same manner, you must earn your right to the
personal attention of your spiritual teacher and to the means
of contact. A good clue to the method lies in our previous statement that you must satisfy the requirements of *this* world before you are privileged to enjoy the fellowship and help of the
unseen world.

This demonstrates again the simple truth of the undivided wholeness of your being. Anything that improves one
area of your life will work to the benefit of all the other areas.
There are no isolated compartments in your existence. The
most intelligent approach to contacting your spiritual teacher
is to set about putting your whole life in order. As you acquire
self-discipline, perspective, and control of your emotions, you
become a spiritual magnet, drawing the teacher closer to you.
Then when your mind is quiet, you will recognize the first faint
manifestations of contact.

Why Contact Requires
Perseverance

The first contacts will be a stern test for your patience
and perseverance. You will get one or two excellent manifestations followed by long periods of agonizing nothingness. Your
ability to receive from your teacher will have all the stability
of a rowboat in a hurricane. Often you will wonder if you have
gone completely mad, but this, too, is a growth process, and it
cannot be accelerated by pulling the petals off the rosebud.
Patience balanced by quiet enthusiasm is your only key.

The practical rewards for this effort more than compensate for the agony. We can see this clearly in the Master's statement of law: *"Seek ye first the kingdom of heaven and all things*

will be added unto you." As you learn to receive clear guidance and tangible help from your teacher, doorways to accomplishment will swing open—opportunities for growth and expression you never dared dream of will seem to just happen to you. This is the logical result of cooperation with the evolutionary plan of the universe. *You will live in the light!*

Live in the Light, Always

There remains only the purchase of an "insurance policy." The prudent man wants to insure that he will continue to live in the *light* for the remainder of this and any future incarnations. The price of the policy is obvious when you recall the law of attraction and repulsion. What you give you have, and what you withhold you lose. You insure that you will always live in the *light* by continuously sharing it.

How shall you share it? First recall the admonition of the Master, *"Cast not your pearls before swine."* Let's translate that into modern language as, "don't make yourself obnoxious by preaching the higher life and the unseen world to people who are too engrossed in the material to understand."

Be tactful and versatile in your striving to share the *light* with others. If you blurt out the conclusion without first carefully laying the foundation and selling the premise, you will only drive reasonable men away from your light.

In general, you should drop only very subtle hints of the great truths you have made a part of you. Make your own life the example of productiveness and well-being which will inspire men to inquire into the nature of the power you possess. Even in answer to direct questions, be tactful. Many are not ready for the whole teaching and would recoil, branding you "some kind of a nut." You haven't shared your *light* if your words alienated the questioner. Rather, that is withholding it. Seek always to share, but with enough intelligence to get positive results.

The reward is worth all your effort. It is fulfillment, your highest happiness, the peace that passeth all understanding, and graduation from the school of earth life.

Now—Begin Growing Today

We opened Chapter One by asking you to write your answer to a question about the pyramids. Before you go looking for that piece of paper, ask yourself again: Were the pyramids of Egypt really built by thousands of man-years of slave labor, or were they

chapter fourteen

built by some other power held secret in the hearts of men? Now compare your two answers. Is there a significant difference? If so, you have already been rewarded for your effort—and it should be showing tangible results in your life.

I wondered if my personal answer would change during the writing of this book, and I am happy to report that it did, although I would use almost identical words to express it. Obviously my approach is pragmatic, so my answer is: It doesn't matter to me, here and now, how the pyramids were built. They might have been built by either method. What does matter is I *know* there is a very real power working in my life which *will* accomplish any goal, providing I am willing to pay its price. And the price is always the giving of myself, in attention, love, and work for the idea.

This all ties in with the *use of your* GOD-POWER to establish the new beginning. We will let the idea slowly unfold as we pick up the questions left over from Chapter Fourteen.

We left three main points to be examined here:

1. Why should a grown man want to take a picture of a discarnate entity or spirit?

2. Is it possible to objectively measure a subjective experience such as contact with a spiritual teacher?

3. How can I objectively value the help of my spiritual teachers on a project like this book?

Looked at together, these are obviously degrees of only one basic problem. Its most straightforward definition is: Where is there a *positive* link between the objective and subjective worlds?

The Eastern philosophies avoid the problem by defining the objective world as Maya, or illusion. But you and I can't buy that one, if for no other reason than it still hurts when we sit on a thumbtack. The Western world tends toward the opposite approach that it is the subjective world which is illusion. However the very existence of psychosomatic medicine proves the subjective must have some reality. Where is the point of balance?

Since we live in the West and have been taught the reality of the material world from birth, our starting point must be the objective. We have lived our whole life out of balance on the material end of the seesaw. But we have it within us to climb to the balance point, if only we can sense its direction. Again our indicators must come from that which we already know.

The Imbalance of the Physical Sciences

Physical science seems to believe there is no God unless He can be demonstrated in a test tube. Great scientists have probed deep into the heart of matter-energy attempting to discover its reality, but their seeking has only increased our fund of knowledge about the *material manifestations* of God. It has left us completely ignorant of God Himself. Others, such as Dr. Rhine at Duke, have contributed much to our understanding of ESP which is a bridge between the two worlds. But even they have been limited by socio-academic pressures and the rigors of the so called scientific approach.

The Imbalance of Religion

On the other hand, our basic religions have gone merrily along picturing God as an old man with a long white beard who sits on a throne far away, judging the actions of men and plotting terrible punishments for our transgressions. In the last century, under a broad category we might call neo-Hegelianism, there has arisen a series of "new thought" movements such as Christian Science, Divine Science, Religious Science, Spiritual Science, and hundreds of lesser personality cults. All of these have sought to bridge the gap to the material world, but they have generally fallen into one or both of two traps. Either they oversimplify God and the creative process, or they over-complicate the thought processes. New Thought has done much good, but it has also alienated many seekers by its almost "goody-goody" attitudes.

If science is too cold, and religion is too head-in-the-clouds or goody-goody, where do we look for our link? The fringes of science and religion have groped towards each other for many years. Enough progress has been made that we are nearing the day of their meeting, the discovery of the point of balance between them. It is the culmination of that link-up which I suggest as the new beginning we seek.

There is a significant opportunity for a few people to make an unusual contribution to the advancement of mankind by bringing to fruition this link-up of science and religion. The union is inevitable; it is simply a matter of time. But think of the millions of seekers who could be saved from untold suffering if this merger could be consummated fifty or a hundred years sooner than it would by the present groping process! Here is a dream which is intensely practical—one that might be realized in our lifetime.

It is reasonable for a pragmatist to harbor a vision so long as he keeps one foot planted firmly on the ability to achieve. Join this devout pragmatist as he pauses to share his most cherished dream with you.

Building a New Kind of Organization

As science and religion stumble nearer to each other, there is a growing need for a new kind of organization—a living, vibrant group unhampered by the rigors of academic pressures and the scientific approach or the doctrines and dogma of traditional religion. With balance, energy, and carefully selected personnel, the organization will be in a position to bridge the gap. It must plant itself squarely between science and religion, toss a rope to each, and pull them together.

The scope and approach of the group should be unlimited. There are many avenues to unity, and each bears detailed investigation. Much will be done with ESP, but there may be more promise in the physics of light, in nuclear physics, or in plain old-fashioned metaphysics.

The physics of light may lead us into a complete understanding of the *aura* and revolutionize diagnostic medicine as a by-product. Nuclear physics could finally contact the intelligence behind the manifestation of living matter and thus meet God face to face. Or, group practice of metaphysics might bring personal visits from the Master to continue and modernize His teachings. After all, He did leave us the promise: *"For where two or three are gathered together in my name, there am I in the midst of them."* (Matt. 18:20)

The Dawn of a New Age

The possibilities of bringing *good* to the world through such an organization are unlimited. Mankind may be uplifted for all time by the work to come out of this group. The astrological world tells us we are on the cusp of a new age. We are moving from the Piscean to the Aquarian way of manifestation, and to the astrologers' way of thinking this includes linking the objective with the subjective.

There is something intrinsically sound in astrology, but its practitioners are working in near-darkness. Perhaps a large analog computer could be programmed to study this near science which has already given us the respected science of astronomy. We have the intellectual and technological capability to delve into the depths of astrological lore and make a useful tool out of it. Why not try?

Astrology naturally leads us into the broad field of divination which includes numerology, tarot, the various oracles, palmistry, phrenology, the art of dowsing, aura reading, psychometry, I Ching, and many more. These "pseudo-sciences" have been maintained by their bands of devoted followers for many centuries. The intellectual world is quick to criticize these sects for their obvious shortcomings, but the mere fact of their longevity indicates there must be something there. What is it?

Let's find out! But our approach will have to be free from prejudice, either for or against. The presence of crackpots and charlatans doesn't necessarily mean there is no value in their field of endeavor. Even the modern medical profession hasn't been able to completely rid itself of "screwballs" and racketeers. But no one in his right mind would condemn all doctors because of the malevolent activities of the very few. Economics wasn't much of a science before Adam Smith. We need a few twentieth century Adam Smiths to turn more borderline activities into acceptable professions. How can we *know* the truth until we create an atmosphere unfettered by conformist thinking?

Filling the Void

Shall we seek a name for the organization which will create this unconditioned atmosphere? I think not. The name is relatively unimportant, but the *function* needs to be performed—the *void needs to be filled*. What is your part in such an undertaking? This you must answer for yourself.

The need is more pressing than space exploration or interplanetary travel, and it is worth the expenditure of funds of the same magnitude. However, this is not the type of project which lends itself readily to government financing or control. If the organization is to be truly effective, it must remain free from the red tape and huge procedures manuals so typical of the big government operation.

The Material Requirements

The need is for an extremely informal, university-type atmosphere which can attract men of high caliber. With adequate funding, top flight people will be guaranteed a reasonable financial future. Thus, their minds can be freed from the pressures of money-grubbing, and they will be capable of the mental and spiritual growth so necessary to the success of the undertaking. We have already done this for our missile and space scientists. Why not try it to advance the spiritual also?

The people who dedicate themselves to this momentous project will need the tools of their trade. The focal point of activity should be a campus complete with offices, conference rooms, laboratory equipment, digital and analog computers, thinking rooms, a large meeting place, a large library, and perhaps living quarters. The extremities of its operation and influence would be infinite.

Where shall we find the funds, personnel, and real estate? Right now that's God's business! Our part is to build a new personal beginning by giving of our prayers for the new group. We will use the Formula for Personal Creation as a mass method to bring the organization which will link science and religion into physical plane manifestation.

Join me in this last use of the formula together. Let it be your final review of this work and a graduation gift from you to the world. Step by step, let's now build the new beginning.

We have studied God's purpose and agreed it is *evolution*. This is true as regards any individual and even more powerfully true as it embraces the whole species of man. Let each of us pledge his whole being to the Divine Plan of Evolution, *now!*

We have just united with God's personal plan of creation. We have consciously joined God's team. *God is on our side!* And if God be for us, who can be against us? We may falter or stumble, but He has given his angels charge over us to guard us in all of our ways. Truly, they will bear us up in their hands, lest we strike even our foot upon a stone. We will not fail God, and He cannot fail us.

Watch out for that little doubt about your own importance. Your individual prayer or treatment is vitally important to the success of the whole organization and to your own progress. Enter into the mental work with enthusiasm!

Focus your GOD-POWER by visualizing the result—the physical manifestation of our shared dream. Realize the full import of linking the subjective and objective. It is the culmination of science and religion. It is full understanding of how the universe really functions, and consequently a cure for all disease and a source of all supply. It is everyman's dream of Utopia, but it is not an end in itself. It is only the beginning of a new age of growth and progress. We are not intellectually capable of predicting what the next goal will be, but we are sure it will be as far above our present goal as this goal is above the world we live in today.

Pour out your love upon this glorious vision of the union of science and religion. Love it, live it, work for it any way that appeals to you. Now apply your focused GOD-POWER directly to the problem area. Say aloud:

"I trust in God with all my heart and He directs my growth in the Christ Idea. He is giving birth to an effective organization to unite religion and science into a living, vibrant organism, now. Thank you, Heavenly Father, for this perfect gift to mankind."

Release It to God—
Results Follow

Use the treatment regularly. "I trust in God with all my heart and He directs my growth in the Christ Idea. He is giving birth to an effective organization to unite religion and science into a living, vibrant organism, now. Thank you, Heavenly Father, for this perfect gift to mankind."

Release it to God after each affirmation. If you feel impelled to take further action, by all means do so, but your very act of regularly praying for mankind's new beginning is the creation of your own highest good.

According to the law of attraction and repulsion, the act of striving to bring the new beginning to mankind assures you of a new personal beginning. Accept it and start another round of evolution on the higher level. The peace that passeth all understanding is yours as you consciously cooperate with the evolutionary process. Enjoy it! Share it! Rejoice as you see all mankind moving upward along the great spiral of growth.

Every achievement is a base for the beginning of greater achievement. *Grow* into your highest happiness!

I invite correspondence from any who are sincerely interested in building an organization such as has been outlined.

May your fondest dreams of today be the realities of your tomorrow. *Use* what you have learned and it *is* so!